THE SEASONS

THAT SHAPED ME

A JOURNEY OF GRIEF, HEALING, AND LEARNING TO BLOOM AGAIN

THE SEASONS
THAT SHAPED ME

A JOURNEY OF GRIEF, HEALING, AND LEARNING TO BLOOM AGAIN

A Memoir

ANGIE LEA

The Seasons That Shaped Me.

A journey of grief, healing and learning to bloom again by Angie Lea

Published by Angie Lea

www.AngieLea.com

Copyright © 2025 Angie Lea

Cover and Book Design by Angie Lea

ISBN: 979-8-9990285-0-1

Angie Lea

Printed in United States of America

First Edition

My dear reader, this story is rooted in truth as I have lived and remembered it. To honor the privacy of others: names, places, and details have been gently reshaped or blended. Memory is a living, breathing thing—shifting like seasons—and while this is my truth, others may remember it differently. This memoir is offered with love, reflection, and deep respect for all who have walked beside me.

To the ones who held space when the storms came:
family, friends, and my steadfast therapist.
Thank you for staying when the winds howled.

To those who walked beside me,
on meandering forest trails, up tall mountains,
through silence, wonder, and shared breath.
Thank you for those moments of connection.

To the seasons that shaped me,
the trails that taught me to trust,
and this tender, stubborn heart
that kept choosing love through grief.

For the ones who have lost,
who have hurt,
and who kept going anyway,
this is for you.

Just like moons and like suns,
With the certainty of tides,
Just like hopes springing high,
Still I'll rise.

Maya Angelou, "Still I Rise"

Contents

Chapter 1

Love Blooms

A warm breeze fluttered the white curtains by the open window, and sunlight danced in the corners as it peeked through the tall evergreen trees in my yard. The breeze carried soft birdsong and the distant low hum of a lawn mower to my ears.

Summer. My favorite season. The days were longer and brighter, my feet lighter as the warm air infused me with a feeling of weightlessness.

I sank into my hand-me-down, oversized ivory love seat facing the window. My feet tucked beneath me, I soaked in the warmth of summer's promise as it whispered gently through the curtains. The whisper promised warmth, but little did I know that it was also bringing profound change.

I took a deep breath. The faint scent of grass filled my mind with nostalgic childhood memories.

I admired the bright yellow sunflowers on the windowsill. The long stems rested in a white milk glass vase that I had purchased at a garage sale for a quarter. I thought, *Such a simple pleasure, having flowers in the window.*

The breeze lifted a strand of my long, dark brown hair over my cheek. The light tickle made me tuck it behind my ear. I glanced at the clock on the wall. My quest would start soon, and I needed to join my friends.

I stood, stretched my long arms above my head to touch the ceiling, and smiled. I opened the slatted doors of the tall espresso armoire, revealing my computer and stacks of homework papers. The furniture loomed large in the small rental house with its lettuce- and aloe-green walls. This space held more than electronics and schoolwork—it was my gateway to another world.

Every evening, the moment I opened those doors, reality faded. The armoire transformed from a simple storage unit into a portal. It was a threshold between the ordinary and magical. On one side, I was Angie, a thirty-one-year-old single mother, a college student, a woman navigating life's uncertainties. On the other side, I became something else: powerful, magical, free. This space, this screen, allowed me to slip into a world where I could be carefree.

The computer screen flickered to life. My high elf character appeared at the mouth of a cave beneath a rocky cliff. Storm clouds gathered overhead. Her blonde hair flowed past pointed ears, and her purple-and-gold robe shimmered with magic.

I summoned my pet familiar, which I had amusingly named Cookies. I was often amused by the quirky, imaginative world I found in online role-playing games like this.

Our group needed a fighter to lead the charge. Minutes passed before a message popped up: "I'm a fighter; I can help."

I clicked the fighter's stats: Barbarian Monk. An odd combination. Barbarians relied on brute strength, monks on agility. I hesitated, but with no better options, I sent the invite.

Inside the cave, ogres attacked immediately. The monk fought with precision, his movements swift and deliberate. He was clever, funny, and skilled.

"Anyone want some Cookies?" I quipped, sending my minion into battle.

Our healers worked relentlessly. Light flashed around us as we pushed through the dark underworld. Finally, we reached a vast cavern.

A dragon emerged from the shadows.

This was it.

We fought as a team, each move precise. Moments later, the dragon lay motionless. Victory. We collected our treasures and parted ways.

"Good fighter," I noted in my book, making a mental note to call on him again.

I played a role, living in a world of magic. A tall high elf with blonde hair, blue eyes, and a robe imbued with magical enchantments. A conjurer from a distant land with a whimsical, playful nature. When asked where I was from, I spun elaborate tales, and I would laugh and pretend not to know what "real life" was.

I was cleverly hidden behind a protective veil where no one could see the real me.

The day after slaying the dragon, my character rode upon a valiant ivory horse. Its silky mane flowed in the pixelated grasslands. The blonde me paused to pick up sticks, plants, and rocks.

Real me felt uninterested in the sticks and rocks in the game and felt a pull to go out into the real outdoors to enjoy real nature. I felt tired of pretending that day. I let out a sigh as my character got off her horse and bent to gather a rock and place it in her leather satchel. I wondered what else I could do with my day, bored of the monotony.

I heard the distinct ping of an incoming chat message. It was the Barbarian Monk.

He asked, "What are you doing?"

"I'm listening to music and harvesting. What about you?" I replied, surprised that I had strayed from character.

"I'm listening to music and killing some skeletons in a cave. What are you listening to?"

I hesitated, tempted to go back into character. "Oh, I'm listening to Nickelback."

He responded, "Me too!"

"Which song?" I asked.

"Far Away," he replied.

"Me too!" I exclaimed.

I hesitated. *What are the odds?* My character stood by her horse as we exchanged messages about music, our favorites overlapping. A connection sparked.

"What's your real name?" he asked.

My fingers hovered over the keys. "Angie," I typed. "Yours?"

I paused. I never gave out my real name. Something told me it was okay this time, and I pressed send.

Seconds later: "Hi, Angie! I'm Nate."

I smiled.

The weeks that followed blurred into endless conversations. We dug deep with a thirst to know what made each other light up about life, family, friends. We shared our thoughts on the world. We made each other laugh with silly jokes and gentle playfulness. A connection spanned two thousand miles. Each evening, we chatted on the phone, excited to share our day's details. After hours of conversation, we would fade to gentle whispers as our eyes became heavy.

We had our first date across the miles. He was in Ohio, where he lived. I was in Washington, where I lived. We pressed our flip phones to our ears and watched our favorite movie, *The Princess Bride*, while eating bags of Swedish Fish candy and microwave popcorn.

"Farm boy . . . fetch me that pitcher." I giggled, listening through the phone to see if our DVDs were in sync.

"As you wish," he whispered.

"Inconceivable!" I exclaimed.

"Death cannot stop true love. All it can do is delay it for a while," he repeated.

I observed Nate that summer. I noticed how he interacted with others in the game—kind, considerate. I noticed how he interacted with me—tender, empathetic, caring. With each moment of tenderness and consideration, my feelings grew deeper. I knew this wasn't just infatuation. It was real. Love had quietly taken root and begun to bloom. There was a feeling of safety in being vulnerable. I felt like I could share those parts of me that I had carefully hidden for so long.

I had no idea how it was possible to fall deeply for a man I hadn't even met in person, but I had. I was curious if he had felt it too.

One evening, my phone rang.

"I have something important to tell you." There was a smile in his voice.

"Oh?" I knew what he was about to say.

The call dropped, and I redialed. "What were you going to say?"

I hoped I was right. I wanted him to say it.

"I love you, Angie."

I felt it too. "I love you too, Nate."

I let out a deep sigh of contentment. I was glad that he felt the same way.

Summer had transformed me, melting away the layers I'd hidden behind. The game, once a sanctuary, faded gently like the last rays of sunset, replaced by something far more real and profound— connection, trust, and vulnerability. Love became the gentle sunlight that warmed my hidden truths, inviting me to step from the shadows of my carefully crafted character. With Nate, I didn't just feel seen; I felt accepted, cherished exactly as I was. The masks fell away, revealing a self I'd nearly forgotten. For the first time, I could breathe deeply, knowing I was safe, knowing I was enough. Love allowed me to fully bloom, embracing the real me beneath the mask.

Chapter 2
Love Grows

As the sunflowers of summer turned to asters and chrysanthemums of autumn, I waited outside Sea-Tac Airport baggage claim. The warmth of early October still lingered. I fixed my eyes on the arrival screen. Nate's flight had landed. Butterflies stirred in my stomach. I wiped my sweaty palms on my jeans and adjusted my white short-sleeve sweater over my teal-blue tank top. I wondered: Would I recognize him? Would he still like me in person? He knew I was taller than he was, so I wore flats. Would he care? I hoped he would accept me for who I was in person, as much as he had accepted me through our interactions over the phone.

Doubts nagged, and my friends' warnings echoed: *What if he's not who he says he is?* I had been honest, but could I trust that he had also been honest?

My mom's words steadied me: *When you know, you know. Everything else is a waste of time.* Nate and I had talked for months, exchanged "I love you" many times. I knew.

Then I saw him. His eyes met mine, his face lit up, and suddenly we were the only two people in that airport. His short, blond curls slicked down, his blue eyes bright, his muscular arms exposed beneath rolled-up sleeves. He dropped his dark green duffel bag and pulled me into a tight embrace. I melted into his arms.

We left the airport, and I drove my little red Ford Focus home. My fingers touched the edge of the bouquet of flowers that sat between us, a gift he had purchased at the kiosk on the way out of the airport. I smiled, and my eyes met his. He was looking at me too, grinning. "I never want to stop looking at you!" he said, reaching to touch my shoulder and gently moving his fingertips to my hand. Electricity flowed between us.

His gaze shifted outside the driver's side window. "Look at that tree!" He pointed toward a tree growing alongside the freeway.

I giggled at the awe in his voice. "That's a freeway tree! Wait until you see the big ones!"

"They get bigger than that?" he gasped.

I grinned. "I can't wait to show you!"

We explored Washington together over the next week. We hiked through evergreen forests and stood at the edge of the Pacific Ocean. His eyes widened as cold ocean waves lapped at his feet for the first time. He plucked a dandelion and tucked it behind my ear. "Angie, my sweets," he whispered, kissing my forehead, my nose, my lips, "I am so happy to be here with you."

He met my parents, their spouses, my younger sister, and my best friend Kristen. I saved meeting my son for a future visit. Every moment felt too short. At the airport, I clung to him, tears already falling as he opened the car door to make his way to his gate. As I drove home, "Chasing Cars" played on the radio, and I reflected on that morning in my mind. His arms around me, the same song had played softly on the radio. By the time he landed in Ohio, I had already booked my flight to see him.

Two weeks later, I was in Nate's arms again. This time, we were on his turf. He showed me his world. He shared his family and their sixteen-acre farm, the hobbit-like house with its grass roof, and the pond where we fished for bass with long cane poles.

Each morning, he brought me coffee, traced my face with his fingertips, memorizing every bit of me. "The apartment is yours. I'll be home at three."

I curled up in his bed, sipped the coffee, and watched golden leaves outside the window. A squirrel darted through the branches. "That's Skippy, the acrobatic squirrel!" I laughed, remembering our calls and his fond descriptions of Skippy. This was real. He was real.

Afternoons, he swept me into dips and kisses. Evenings, we cooked together or dined at his favorite spots. Every touch, every glance confirmed what we had felt across the miles.

The week vanished. At the airport, we planned our next visits. November, when he would meet my son. December, when he would meet more family and friends at my mom's annual Christmas party.

We knew. We had always known.

The day after Christmas, I flew to Ohio with a one-way ticket. It felt exciting and scary at the same time. I wouldn't be returning to Washington by plane. I would be returning in Nate's truck, with him by my side.

That evening, the chill of Midwest December couldn't dim our spirits as we gathered at his mom's house. The warm glow of her beautiful home surrounded us. His remaining belongings were stacked by the door in large black trash bags.

As the last visitors left that evening, we climbed the stairs to the second-floor guest room. I sat on the bed, my legs folded under me, and handed him a package wrapped in white-and-gold paper, tied with brown twine.

His eyes lit up. "Oh! What's this?"

"Open it." I grinned, shifting with excitement.

He carefully peeled back the paper. He held the black leather scrapbook, his hands pausing before opening the cover. It was filled with photos from our short time together. Printed pictures and mementos, paired with burnt CDs of songs capturing our love story.

"We can listen to the CDs on the drive to Washington!" I said, flipping to the back. "And fill these pages with new memories!"

He thumbed through the book, chuckling at our photos. Leaning in, he kissed me. "Thank you. I can't wait!"

As we turned out the light and pulled the covers over us, I felt excited for the life that awaited us.

"Angie?" I heard him whisper in the dark.

"Nate?" I whispered back.

"I love you," he whispered. "I'm so excited for the adventures ahead of us."

"I love you too," I replied. "And me too, so very much."

I smiled in the dark. He pulled me close and wrapped his arms around me. I felt the warmth of his love. I felt safe. I felt comforted.

Nate and I drove across the country together, a start of our new shared adventure. We alternated between karaoke with the scrapbook CDs and deep conversations about life. We pulled over at every state line to kiss, each kiss longer and more intense. We stopped at roadside attractions—the Corn Palace, Wall Drug, Mount Rushmore.

Snow blew sideways across the highway, hovering above the ground, refusing to settle. At night, snowy blizzards turned the dark road into a tunnel. The white snow was like swirling stars. As if time-traveling to a whole new galaxy beyond what either of us could imagine.

We reached Washington just in time to ring in the New Year. Together.

Weekends became a blend of carefully planned and impulsively spontaneous adventures: road trips, hikes, museums, camping, and ocean visits. Some weekends, we simply drove with no destination. We let curiosity or a flipped coin decide on our route. He always drove; I rode shotgun.

We explored the hidden corners of the Pacific Northwest through each season. Autumn discoveries in small-town bakeries with the scent of fresh bread. Winter warm-ups at tea shops, lifting our pinkies to sip and savor. Springtime road trips with quirky roadside diners as we chased blooming flowers. Long days of summer sandcastles and indulging our craving for sweets with candy shops and saltwater taffy.

Nate, having spent most of his life in Ohio, marveled at the towering mountains and dense forests. I grew up in the Pacific Northwest. I had forever loved the variety of nature spaces, but they had lost the vibrancy they once had. His wonder rekindled my childhood joy, my memories of alpine lakes, autumn hikes, snowy bike rides on logging roads, and springtime gardens.

Nate saw beauty in everything, and in me. I felt his adoration toward me when I was happy and beaming, and also when I retreated into sadness. He'd wrap me in his arms and whisper, "I've got you." His presence was my refuge. I could be real. I could be vulnerable. I could be all parts of me. He accepted it all and held space for me with compassion and empathy.

He noticed the little things.

He noticed that the blaring alarm clock startled me in the mornings. His solution was to wake up just before the alarm, turn it off, and go downstairs to make coffee. Each morning, he would kneel at my bedside, a steaming mug of coffee cupped between his hands. He would gently blow the scent toward me until my eyes fluttered open. "Your coffee, my sweets," he'd say, pressing a kiss to my forehead.

The smell of the coffee would fill my lungs and my eyes would open. "Thank you," I'd reply, smiling with so much appreciation.

"As you wish," he'd say with a grin.

It was our morning ritual.

Each morning, I felt so loved and considered. It was his way of setting a beautiful tone for every day. He did it because he knew that it was meaningful to me, and it was meaningful to him that I felt loved. We both felt loved and considered. It was the foundation that we were building on.

But life wasn't always about sweet coffee mornings and road trips.

Nate's ex-wife, Dolores, had moved to Texas with their young daughter, making visitation difficult. They had been unable to agree on a parenting plan during the divorce, and the challenges surrounding that seeped into our lives.

He accepted the occasional phone call, his voice full of adoration. "Daddy loves you!" he'd say, his eyes shining. He wanted more.

Final custody negotiations brought a thick packet of vindictive allegations from Dolores. Claims that painted him as abusive, a man unrecognizable to me. Nate, the gentlest soul I had ever known, didn't fight back. He just wanted to see his daughter, who was only a toddler.

The court ordered six months of supervised visits.

Each month, he flew to Texas to spend time with his daughter. He rented a car, drove for hours, checked into a cheap bed-and-breakfast, then spent two hours in a monitored room playing with his daughter. I stayed home, eagerly waiting for updates.

"Oh, sweets," he'd sigh into the phone, sending me pictures of her tiny arms wrapped around his neck. "She's perfect."

For the last supervised visit, I traveled with him. The visitation center was small. The room had a rocking chair, a table, a few toys, and books. His daughter ran to him, squealing, "Daddy!"

We played. We laughed. Yet the mirrored glass watching us made me uneasy, as if we were criminals.

Nate didn't complain. "I'm just grateful to see her," he told me.

I admired his strength. To him, love was always worth the effort. Love was action. He showed up and followed through each month, despite the toll it was taking financially and emotionally. The staff at the visitation center took note. They told him that he was an amazing dad. He was so kind, so caring, and not someone who needed supervised visitation.

We were both glad that he would finally get to visit her for more than a couple of hours a month and build a stronger relationship with his daughter.

Nate and I got married a year after we drove across the country together at a tiny grange hall on the first day of January with about thirty people in attendance. A light drizzle that morning couldn't dampen our spirits. The tree outside the grange hall reached its bare branches toward the bright gray sky.

Our wedding was small and incredibly low-key, unlike our first weddings. I wore a simple white wedding gown I'd found on a clearance rack at a local bridal boutique. I used a binder clip from my office supply stash to pinch the back together because it was too big. I greeted guests at the door; to their surprise, there was no secret reveal. Just simplicity. Just love.

My son, Max, age nine, walked me down the aisle lined with deep red poinsettia plants. I looked down at Max, and he looked up at me. We had the same brown eyes, same brown hair, although his was spiked up in the front just a little. He smiled sweetly at me and I squeezed his hand as we continued to walk.

The song "From This Moment On" played from the borrowed speakers. Deep red ballet-style shoes hid beneath my long A-line gown and peeked out as I took each step closer to Nate.

Nate caught a tear at the corner of his eye as he watched me approach. The room glowed with warm white lights and candles. The tables were covered in photos of our adventures. Love in every form filled the space.

As the officiant declared us husband and wife, Nate cupped my face tenderly, as if he held my heart itself. Our lips met, sealing a promise that, like the seasons, our love would change but never fade. Through every cycle of warmth and cold, light and darkness, of root and bloom, we would endure.

As our love grew, our uncertainties began to soften, replaced by a deeper knowing. A certainty that grew stronger with every shared laugh, every quiet glance, every whispered dream. We had traded pixelated quests for tangible adventures, each moment spent together further entwining our worlds.

Together, we discovered beauty, not only in sprawling mountains, serene coastlines, and sunlit forests but also in quiet mornings over steaming coffee, in the tender gestures of understanding, and in the comfort of being genuinely seen and accepted, even through life's storms. Through every conversation, every shared silence, every challenge faced hand in hand, we built a foundation rooted deeply in mutual respect, kindness, and love.

And in the gentle glow of winter's promise, we were confident that whatever seasons lay ahead, we would meet them together— hearts open, eyes bright with hope, forever committed to nurturing the life we had so lovingly begun.

Chapter 3
Unexpected Blooms

Nine months after our wedding, the dark green leaves on the paper birch began to turn yellow at the edges. The last bits of summer in the Pacific Northwest gave us warm days of respite before the cold rains set in. Nate and I returned home from the downtown waterfront and farmers market. I pulled the white milk glass vase out of the cupboard for the bouquet of fresh flowers we'd bought from the market.

The phone rang. Nate nudged me and turned the phone so I could see Dolores's name scroll across the screen. I felt my heart rate spike, as it usually did when I saw her name. Nate touched the button on his cell phone to put it on speaker.

"I'm so sorry for keeping our daughter from you," she pleaded, sounding remorseful. "It was my boyfriend's fault. He was the one who wrote the allegations, and he has been more and more abusive, and I've decided to leave him. I want to move to Washington. I've stockpiled money that he gave me for groceries. He agreed to rent me a moving truck."

"Absolutely," Nate replied. "How can we help?"

"Help me find a place to rent there?" she asked.

We nodded at each other as he replied, "We will see what we can find and get back to you soon."

Nate hung up the phone and threw his arms around me. "This is so exciting!" he said.

"Do you think she really will?" We had been waiting for a moment like this. A chance to bring his daughter closer. But my stomach clenched, wondering what the catch was.

"I sure hope so, sweets," he said. "Just got to have faith."

Nate's daughter, Lilly, was four years old. She had her dad's bright blue eyes shining with curiosity. Her sweet face was framed by wisps of light hair that curled slightly at the ends. When she spoke, her voice had a singsong quality, and her laughter filled the room like sunlight. He had satisfied the requirements for supervised visitations, which felt good. But it was increasingly difficult to get access to her without the support of the visitation center to coordinate. Phone calls and visits with Lilly had become less and less welcome. Nate tried to stay connected by mailing books, handwritten letters, and cards. The letters were often returned, unopened, with bold writing on the outside: NO ONE HERE BY THAT NAME.

I saw the hurt on his face each time a letter was returned. I felt angry and confused. I wondered how a parent could keep their child away from their other parent. Especially Nate. He was kind, gentle, and a wonderful stepdad to my son. I would never keep my son from his dad. Regardless of our marriage status, Max needed a relationship with both of us. I couldn't understand the thought process.

We had already prepared a room for Lilly in the house we'd bought a few months before. A bigger house meant that we had space for her too. We dreamed of the day she would be able to come and visit.

Now, there was a possibility of her living close by.

We looked at a furnished one-story rambler on a cul-de-sac ten minutes from our house that was a good match. I felt a mixture of excitement and nausea.

"I'm worried," I said.

"What about?" Nate smiled and touched my arm.

I took a deep breath. I reflected on the constant, erratic phone calls and mood swings from Dolores. The roller coaster of allegations, supervised visitations, returned letters, and packages. I thought about how every time she would call, and I would hear her voice, I would begin to shake. I wondered if it was possible to have PTSD from this woman.

"I am excited to have Lilly down the road, but I'm worried about Dolores being so close. You know the chaos that she causes from a distance. How will it be with her down the road from us?" I felt guilty even expressing my concerns. How could I hold both joy and fear in the same breath?

I knew that Lilly deserved both parents. I also knew her mom made life extra hard for us, and I didn't trust that she had Lilly's best interests at heart.

Nate moved his hand from my arm to my lower back, pulling me close.

"Everything will work out," he reassured me. "We've got each other."

A few weeks later, Dolores arrived at our door, holding Lilly's hand. I felt my insides shake and my hand tremble, but I tried to direct my attention to Lilly.

"Hey, thanks for having her over for the week so I can settle into the new house," Dolores said.

"Absolutely!" Nate exclaimed. Lilly threw her arms around Nate's neck and nuzzled her face into his shoulder.

I smiled at Lilly as she peeked at me. I touched her little fingers and whispered, "Hi, Lilly." I loved to see the tenderness between Nate and Lilly. It was as if no time had passed.

"See you in a week," Nate said as we watched Dolores leave.

For the next week, it felt like a long-awaited dream had finally materialized. Both our children were together under one roof. Their laughter was a song in my heart. It was a beautiful testament to our strong roots that we had nurtured over time and our commitment to love and family. Our family felt complete. In those moments, I clung to fleeting glimpses of peace.

Max gave Lilly horsey rides through the house, making her erupt in belly laughter. We all ate dinner at the table as a family.

We had talked about this moment since the beginning. Merging our lives together, with both of our children present. Reminders that stability was still possible.

One evening that week, I quietly approached the top of the stairs as Nate stood in the kids' bathroom with Lilly. Lilly stood in front of him on a wooden stool, wearing a pink nightgown with pastel flowers. With each brushstroke over her long blonde hair, he smiled and spoke tenderly to her, "I am kind."

"Kind," she repeated. The word was more like grunts and gibberish than the actual word. Her tiny hands shot out with enthusiasm as she attempted to repeat that she was also smart, strong, and brave.

I smiled as they both noticed me outside the bathroom door. They both smiled, and Lilly pulled at the fabric of her nightgown and grunted.

I pressed my hand on the doorframe and grinned. "Do you like your new jammies?"

She smiled, nodded her head, and made happy sounds while she pointed at the flowers.

"Time for stories," Nate said as he lifted her from the stool. He twirled her around before he placed her bare feet on the linoleum of the bathroom floor. Nate paused for a moment as he passed to kiss me and give me a knowing grin. "I love you."

These were the moments I wanted Lilly to remember. Two people who loved each other dearly, who both loved her. We would be her lighthouse, not knowing what storms she had weathered before us. She was here now.

Lilly ran into her bedroom and pulled books from one of her small bookshelves. She jumped onto the small white bed with a new pink-and-green floral quilt. A small collection of plush stuffed animals was propped against the pillow. We had selected furniture, books, clothes, and toys with care, in hopes that someday she would enjoy them. I smiled; my heart was full of love.

"Good night, Lilly!" I smiled as I watched Nate sit next to her and open the book at the top of the pile.

Nate grinned at me, then began to read as I stepped away.

At the end of the week, Nate buckled Lilly into the car seat in her mom's car, and he kissed her cheek. "Bye, Lilly Bug, see you soon!"

Lilly's face looked sad. I wondered if she understood that this wouldn't be like the times when her dad was kept from her. Now, she lived ten minutes away.

Nate put an arm around me, pulling me closer as we watched the car drive away and blew kisses and waved to Lilly.

A couple of days later, Nate received a phone call from Dolores. I heard the familiar voice coming out of the speaker of Nate's cell phone. My shoulders tensed, and I felt the familiar tightness in my chest.

"Wow, she's a different child," she said. "She actually sat at the table and cleared her plate when she was done. She never does that! You are much better parents than I am."

I remained quiet as I took a batch of cookies out of the oven. I caught myself nodding my head and mouthing, "Of course he is."

I took a deep breath. I hated this feeling. I felt angry for all the time she'd kept Lilly from him and for all the distress we had felt. I had to pause and remind myself that she was here now. We needed to figure out how to make this new dynamic work. For Lilly.

Within a week, we received another call from Dolores.

This call would change our lives forever.

"I've decided to move out of state," she said. "Lilly would be better off living with you and Angie."

My eyes were wide and disbelieving.

"Get it in writing," I whispered.

I braced for the joke, the catch, and the inevitable rug pull.

She insisted that she was serious. We had our lawyer draft the papers, worried that she would change her mind. Fifteen days after she moved to Washington, she signed the papers, sold what didn't fit in her car, and left the state.

Our heads spun at the sudden shift. With signed legal documents in hand, Nate had full custody.

Full custody.

As Lilly joined our family permanently, it felt as if our small garden had suddenly expanded, blossoming with vibrant new life. Her arrival was like planting a precious seed we'd long hoped for but weren't quite certain would ever bloom. Now, under one shared roof, our family roots deepened, intertwining and growing stronger together. Each day, love expanded around us—in gentle moments, shared laughter, and quiet bedtime stories that stitched our hearts more closely.

Yet even as gratitude filled our home with warmth, the reality of full custody felt surreal, like an unexpected bloom appearing overnight. Standing in the quiet of our expanded garden, surrounded by this newfound completeness, I felt awestruck. I was profoundly grateful yet still wondering if I was dreaming. Lilly was finally home, our family whole, our garden thriving in ways we'd once only imagined.

Chapter 4
Fragile Roots

The autumn days darkened, and a chill settled in as change took hold. Moments of crisp sunlight and backyard laughter gave way to relentless rain. The last leaves were stripped from the birch trees.

I stood at the sliding glass door, damp cold seeping into my bones. Outside, rain pooled on the patio, tiny plastic animals scattered across the concrete. Typical Pacific Northwest winter. The evergreens in the corner of the yard stood as silent sentinels.

Nate rifled through graded papers at the kitchen counter. He stacked them neatly, pushing them into his laptop bag. He loved his job. He worked with athletes, fueling his fascination with kinesiology. His job teaching in downtown Seattle was a long drive from our home in Olympia. Lately, his evening classes meant I was home alone. I felt overwhelmed.

"Nate," I said, as he zipped his bag, "can you switch your evening classes? I need help around here."

"You know I've tried. No one wants to teach nights, so I have to cover the classes." He grabbed his keys from the hook.

"It's not fair. They cut your pay, added hours, and I'm doing my best, but either I need to drop out of school or I need help."

"No, you need to finish school. We already discussed this. This has always been your dream. When you're done, I'll go for my master's in kinesiology."

He smiled, pulled me close, and kissed my neck. "I'll try again, sweets. I promise."

I watched him leave, his bag over his shoulder. He was trying. We were both trying.

Having Lilly with us was wonderful. It was also exhausting.

At four, she was emotionally unpredictable and intellectually delayed. Our once-quiet home had become a battlefield of mood swings. She brought violent tantrums, and harsh attempts at speech. Within two weeks of moving in with us, she was expelled from two preschools for assault.

Assault.

At age four.

Nate and I both worked during the day, and he worked most evenings. My evenings consisted of kid activities, dinner, bedtime routines, and hoping to prevent major conflicts. Once the kids were in bed, I would start my homework and fall asleep waiting for Nate to get home.

I knew her struggles weren't her fault, but some nights, I felt like I was failing her. Guilt weighed heavily as I lay awake at night, replaying the day's battles.

Her emotions swung wildly. One moment, she was affectionate and imaginative, the next, expressionless or raging. She kicked, hit, and bit me, Nate, Max—anyone in reach. She lifted furniture, slammed it into walls, and could scream for hours. I told myself she just needed time, consistency, and love. I devoured stacks of books searching for answers.

Evenings were the hardest. I had imagined Nate and I parenting together, but instead, I felt alone, exhausted, and defeated.

As the winter rains turned to spring rains, I sat at my desk, opening envelopes with a silver letter opener. Red tulips stretched toward the sun, their pollen dusting the white milk glass vase. I, too, craved warmth, something to lift the weight I carried.

I tallied bills, recording them into my spreadsheet. I had always managed our money. I took classes to learn how to manage finances, pay off debts and save. I learned to stretch every dollar for long-term financial health. Nate spent impulsively with a short-term mindset.

We were short again. Money had always been tight, but now with Nate's pay cut, and needing to pay for childcare for Lilly, I had to get creative.

I reviewed our bank statement line by line, looking for clues about where our paychecks had gone. I noticed frequent stops at McDonald's for his beloved french fries. I shook my head. Always the french fries. Then I noticed a line item for the video game that Nate and I had played when we first met. It had been several years since either of us had played, and I wondered if Nate had subscribed again.

I walked into the living room where Nate sat on the couch with his legs stretched in front of him. He sat with a pen in his mouth, a pile of tests scattered on his legs.

"Can we talk about this charge on the bank statement?" I sat next to him on the couch.

He looked puzzled. "Oh, that's weird. Why would they charge the account after all this time?"

"Are you gaming again?" I asked.

"No, there must be an error. Maybe it's a glitch, and they started charging the account again?" he wondered aloud.

I paused, confused. "Wait, we didn't have this account back then." I took a deep breath. "Are you telling me the truth?"

This wouldn't be the first time Nate lied about gaming. After he moved to Washington, I found out that he was gaming all day while I was at work instead of looking for a job. He'd lied when I questioned him. Back then, I was struggling financially to support Max and me, and I covered Nate financially too. I had told him that if he lied to me again, I wouldn't stay in a relationship with him. He'd apologized and said he wouldn't game anymore, promising there would be no more lies.

Now, years later, I asked him again. "Are you gaming again?"

"Yes," he confessed, his gaze downward.

I felt a knot in my stomach and a lump in my throat. I wondered why he would lie to me. "How long have you been gaming again?" I asked.

He paused as he calculated the timeline.

"I've been gaming for the last year and a half," he admitted. "I was gaming at night when you thought I was working."

"What?" Now my head started to calculate the timeline, and my breath quickened.

A year and a half? He had said he was at work for a year and a half when he wasn't? I couldn't believe it.

"That's about the time that Lilly moved in with us," I said. "Why would you lie to me? You knew I needed you here! I told you I needed help."

He nodded. "I didn't want to lie to you, and I wasn't exactly lying. I would drive to Seattle so I could tell you I made it to work. Then I would drive back to town. I went to a coffee shop to play until it was time for me to come home from work."

I was horrified.

He'd elaborately twisted his lies into partial truths. All to make himself feel less guilty about lying to me. That would have been up to three hours of extra driving each day just to cover up a lie.

"Is this why your paychecks have been lower?" I questioned. "Even though you said you were working more?"

I was upset; my hands shook as I fought back tears. "All those nights I was *begging* you to stay home. I asked you to get another instructor because I needed *help*, and Lilly needed you . . ."—I paused and bit my lower lip, trying not to cry—"and you were playing a stupid video game?"

I was angry, and the tears began to flow. "We needed you," I repeated, my voice quivering as I sobbed. "How could you lie to me for a year and a half?"

The challenges of the last year and a half flashed through my mind. The screaming from Lilly. The exhaustion I felt from the emotional tornadoes. Trying to soothe Max, who had to endure the chaos.

I thought about all the stress I'd taken on while he was playing a stupid video game. I became furious. I didn't know what to do. The last time he lied, I had told him I wouldn't remain in the relationship. I'd put that boundary in place when we were dating. Now, we were five years into our relationship and we'd been married three years.

"I'm sorry, I just didn't know how to tell you." His shoulders slumped and he looked at the floor. "It was just too hard for me to be here; it was hard having Lilly here. I guess I was just trying to escape the responsibility."

"Why did you agree to have her come live here? Why didn't you talk to me about it? This has been hard on us all. You took the easy way out when things got hard!" My heart felt heavy.

I felt the foundation of trust start to dissolve under our feet, the roots shaking and the ground beginning to crack beneath us. How could this man who tenderly held my heart in his hands lie to me? We had established early on that we both valued the importance of honesty.

How did I not know? Was I stupid? If he'd lied about this, what else had he lied about? How come this was the first time it had shown up on the bank statement if it had been a year and a half?

In the days that followed, he continued to bring me coffee in the mornings just as he had for the last five years. I would hear him come into the room, and I'd turn my back. He would place the coffee on the nightstand and then leave. I was angry, and my heart hurt. I left the coffee untouched as a tribute to the ache in my heart. The coffee would disappear, and a fresh one would appear on my nightstand the next morning.

The season felt turbulent. The chill had settled into our home—subtle at first, then impossible to ignore. Lilly's struggles became storms we hadn't anticipated, shaking the branches of our carefully tended garden. Caught between responsibility and avoidance, Nate's presence had slipped quietly away behind a veil of lies. The hours stretched long, burdening my shoulders with a heaviness I wasn't sure I could bear alone. Each morning, the coffee was an attempt to bridge the widening gap, yet my heart felt weighted, uncertain of his sincerity, questioning if trust, once broken, could ever truly mend.

But slowly, with quiet persistence, Nate showed up. Day after day, cup after cup, he demonstrated through small gestures his desire to nurture what had withered. Tentatively, like the first tender shoots of spring emerging after a harsh winter, trust began to take root again.

Each honest conversation, each genuine moment of vulnerability, gradually rebuilt the foundation beneath us. Though fragile, our roots strengthened bit by bit, reminding us that even after deep frost, renewal was possible.

Hope could still grow, and so could we.

Chapter 5
Summer Sweetness

A few months later, the longer days of summer finally came. Sweet, fragrant aromas drifted through the open windows—lavender, peony, and rose. My garden beds were thick with textures and colors. The glorious smells were best left outside, as fragrances didn't agree with my breathing.

I sat on the couch and spun the mouse wheel with my finger; the news feed of social media lit up my laptop screen. A series of pictures: a pile of tiny springer spaniel puppies, their eyes closed, noses pink. Some photos of individual puppies cupped carefully in hands. Cute, tiny heads and paws. I clicked the link to go to my childhood friend's page.

"Sooooo . . . who wants a puppy?" he had posted.

I scrolled through the photos. *Meeeeee!* I thought as my heart fluttered with excitement.

I commented on the post, "They are cute. Are they good hiking dogs when they're older? How's their parents' disposition?"

He responded, "Springers are good everything dogs . . . They love to fetch and swim, and have lots of energy. The parents are both good dogs. Mama is a little overprotective these days, but dad is a big lovable goofball."

I perked up. "Nate!" I shouted. He ran into the living room from the home office. "Look!" I squealed with joy as he got closer, patting the couch beside me. "Puppies! I need a puppy!"

He chuckled. "You *need* one, huh?"

"Yes, I do." I grinned widely and batted my eyelashes.

"We've had a couple of puppies already, and those didn't work out," he reminded me.

"I know, those puppies were for Max, and this one is for me." I shrugged and thought about the two puppies that we had brought home for Max on two occasions upon his request. We'd quickly found out that he was not ready for that responsibility and neither was I.

I had grown up with spaniels, and the cute little faces taunted me through the screen.

"Can we go get one?" I asked.

Nate chuckled. "We can go look."

"And get one!" I laughed playfully.

"We can go look," he replied with a smirk on his face. "Let's go!"

As he steered the silver Ford Focus on a high-priority mission, I set out to list potential names on my phone. "What are some names that you like?" I asked.

"We're just looking," he repeated with a knowing smile.

"I wanna love him and squeeze him and call him George!" I giggled as I continued to stare at the blinking cursor on my phone notepad.

As we entered the house, I noticed the litter of puppies on the living room floor. Each stumbled drunkenly as their tiny bodies discovered the new world around them. I sat on the floor with my legs crossed under me. I touched the top of each head and tiny body with the tips of my fingers. I placed my pointer finger under each chin for a little scratch.

"Which one?" I asked, looking at Nate.

He smiled. "Well, which one do you want?"

I watched the puppies, observed how they played, stumbled, interacted. "I don't know! This is so hard. I like these two." I pointed first at a white-and-brown boy, then a white-and-black girl.

The boy was rambunctious and feisty. He was fun, and I laughed at his playful interactions with the other puppies. The girl, who was also the runt of the litter, wobbled over to me and lay on my lap before quickly falling asleep.

I looked at Nate and smiled.

Nate smiled back. "Looks like someone chose you."

I scooped her up, her body mostly white with little black markings on her back and face. I put her under my nose and took a big sniff. "Ahh! Puppy breath!"

I tucked her into the front of my sweatshirt and zipped it up so her tiny nose stuck out of the top. Nate opened the passenger-side door as I carefully sat down and buckled up.

Nate chuckled as he looked at me from the driver's seat. "Who are you, and what did you do with my wife?"

I laughed. "Apparently, your wife is a dog person now."

Approaching our house, I looked at Nate. "I want to name her Ruby, after my grandma," I said, "as long as my mom is okay with that."

Nate smiled. "I think that's a great idea!"

After a quick call to my mom to announce our new family member, and with her approval of the name, it was official.

Days later, I watched her tiny body navigate over gigantic blades of grass in our backyard. She wobbled into the patch of lavender, and I watched her fall asleep at the base of the woody stems. She had a cute little squirrel-sized face, and it made us all laugh. From that day forward, she became Ruby Squirrelface. She graced our lives and brought back the squeals of laughter and joy in our home. We welcomed the lighthearted distraction of puppy breath kisses and sharp piranha teeth.

Ruby's tiny paws seemed to walk straight into the cracks in our family's foundation, filling the spaces with warmth and joy. She was the sweet, healing hope we needed that summer. The reminder to bring our perspective back to the things that mattered.

The seasons passed, each with its own lessons, struggles, and shifts. Lilly's arrival upheaved our lives. Responsibilities stretched us thin. Trust fractured. But still, we moved forward—sometimes reluctantly, sometimes painfully, always clinging to hope.

As summer settled in, I found solace again in the small things: our children's laughter, blooming flowers, the soft weight of a puppy curled against my chest.

It was a season wrapped in golden stillness. A lingering sweetness where time seemed to slow, cradling us in warmth and quiet joy. The days stretched long and honeyed, each moment suspended like ripened fruit on the vine, too perfect to last. Beneath the soft hum of summer's embrace, there was an almost faint tension in the air, like the sky holding its breath before the first crack of thunder. We lived in the pause. Savoring the light. Unaware of how quickly the winds could shift, how soon the storm would come.

Chapter 6

The Storm

Two weeks after Ruby's gotcha day, I leaned toward Nate in the kitchen as he playfully kissed me. The warm summer air came in through the open windows and carried the familiar hum of summertime in a small neighborhood.

I thought about how grateful I was that life felt balanced again. Nate and I had reconnected with morning coffee dates and honest heartfelt conversations. Trust grew day by day as we both showed up to be present and honest in our lives. Our little family felt a bit more at peace than it had in a long time.

I smiled as I looked around, the house filled with happy sounds. Lilly's sweet voice sang to her stuffed animals around the dining room table as she poured each animal a cup of tea in tiny white porcelain cups with saucers to match. Max played dance games on his Xbox in the living room with a group of neighborhood friends. The music caused Nate to grab my hands and twirl me in place as I erupted with laughter.

Nate and I spent that afternoon learning to pressure can homemade soup. The sound of steam rocked the round metal weight on top of the pressure cooker as Nate put his arms around me and sweetly kissed my nose.

Ruby was asleep, her belly exposed, legs sprawled, and paws extended over the edge of her small pink bed with white polka dots.

I smiled, content.

Everything was going to be okay.

The next day at work, I stood at the window of my corner office and admired the deep blue sky of a Washington summer, the sun warming my face.

"It's such a beautiful day!" I said to Carol, my work assistant, who had become a trusted friend. "I'm going for a walk," I continued, looking at the time. Just in time for an afternoon break to soak in the picturesque day.

I walked swiftly around the loop, my lungs filled with the sweet scents from the tree-lined streets. I paused at the playground near my office building for a quick swing as I did on many occasions, my feet extended to the sky, my head tipped back, as I went higher and higher, tapping into the simplicity of playful moments. These playful moments made me feel lighter and helped release stress from my day. As the birds sang their songs in the nearby tree and distant sounds of lawn mowers hummed, I thought about how grateful I was.

My cell phone rang—it was Carol. "You need to get back to the office right away," she said quickly.

I ran up the back stairwell and opened my office door.

"What's wrong?" I blurted as I tried to catch my breath.

"Nate's work called; they said he collapsed at work. They called an ambulance and he's on the way to the hospital," Carol explained.

I made calls to arrange childcare and headed to Seattle to the hospital. I fought traffic for over an hour, my mind racing with stories.

Nate could be dramatic when he was sick. Was he just being overdramatic? A wave of panic washed over me as I remembered the soup we'd canned the night before.

"The soup had better not give us botulism," he'd joked. It was our first time canning, and he had taken a can of the soup for lunch.

At the hospital, I checked in at the front desk and I was directed to a waiting room. I felt as if I was trapped inside a cloud, my head a swirl of worried thoughts. Unable to achieve full breaths, my heart raced as I hoped desperately that he was okay.

A doctor appeared in front of me. "Your husband has a perforated ulcer in his duodenum," he explained. "The duodenum is part of the small intestine that connects to the stomach. The ulcer caused it to split open. We are prepping him for surgery, and we will update you when we are done."

"Okay," I replied, relieved that it wasn't botulism but worried about the health of his insides.

I sat alone in the waiting room and made a few calls. I checked in with my mom, who had picked up the kids after school, then called Nate's family in Ohio to relay what the doctor had told me.

I walked to the tall, expansive windows near the waiting room, scared to go far. The summer sky turned dark across the Seattle skyline, and the lights across town created a big city glow that drowned out any chance of seeing the stars.

I wandered back to the waiting area and sat down, and I noticed the doctor approaching.

I smiled nervously. "All done?"

"Yes," he began, his stoic face not providing any sign of emotion. He sat down in the chair next to me. "While we were in there, we found tumors on his liver. It's a rare cancer called carcinoid. Unfortunately, it is terminal and there is no cure."

My head felt like it was wrapped in bubble wrap. I gripped the arms of my chair; my world began to spin. *Terminal? What does that even mean?* The word kept repeating in my head. "You mean, he isn't going to live? How long does he have?"

The doctor looked at me and said, "We aren't sure. We will have to do more tests."

He paused; did he say something else? I stared up at him, my insides shaking. Was I also shaking on the outside? The doctor left me there in the waiting room. I was alone.

Nate is only thirty-six years old—we both are. That's too young.

I couldn't breathe. No. It couldn't be true. *Why did the doctor just leave me alone here? Where did he go? I'm all alone!* I began to sob.

The evening became a blur. I vaguely remember calling my mom, and at some point, my aunt and uncle arrived. Did I call them or did she?

I saw Nate. The doctors had told me he knew, but he didn't seem to know what I was talking about. He was scared. I was scared.

Later, I couldn't recall how I got home.

Nate was in the hospital for ten days after his surgery, and our lives quickly became a series of oncologist appointments and hospital stays. At his first oncologist appointment, we learned more about his cancer. Nate had a carcinoid tumor that was a type of neuroendocrine tumor.

"The tumors are often so slow to grow, and people might have them and die of natural causes before knowing they had them," the oncologist explained. "The cancer is so rare, and has nothing to do with genetics, lifestyle, or health. It's just a one-in-a-million fluke."

I clung to the words "slow to grow" and hoped that was the case for Nate, that he would have an opportunity to live a full life.

I quickly absorbed as much information as I could and typed detailed notes on my iPad of everything the oncologist said so I could look up words I didn't know, remember them, and do more research later. We were flooded with information, and it was overwhelming. I asked questions about everything and wanted answers to somehow make sense of it all.

Nate and I watched documentaries and read books and felt inspired by holistic health and the possibility of healing the cancer. We both started juicing daily and living a more plant-based lifestyle at the recommendation of the Gerson therapy model of healing. Nate was confident that with the elimination of his regular beloved supersized french fries and sugary weekend cheat meals he would be cured in no time.

In September, two months after his diagnosis, we sat in the corner of the waiting room of the oncology office. The charcoal-colored fabric of the upholstered chair beneath me, I looked around the room at the others waiting. I wondered what they were going through and thought about the harsh reality of cancer for almost everyone I knew.

Previous test results had showed no change in the tumors.

My gaze shifted to Nate. He looked good; he appeared healthy, as he always had. He flexed his arm at me and winked. If anyone could beat the cancer, it would be Nate. He was a fighter. The man had earned two black belts, he could wield a samurai sword, and he regularly took care of his physical body through exercise and movement. He was strong.

I wanted to capture this moment. "Say cheese," I said, lifting my phone to snap a picture.

Nate raised his hands, giving me two thumbs-up as I took the photo.

A woman appeared through the door of the waiting room with a clipboard and called his name. I looked at him and I felt nervous.

He flashed a big smile. "I've absolutely got this!" he exclaimed.

I felt comforted by his optimism. "Of course, you do!" I smiled back as Nate disappeared beyond the waiting room doors.

We thought summer was wrapping us in tender stillness. Each day was unfolding like a soft promise that maybe, just maybe, we had weathered our hardest seasons. Love lingered in the air like the sweetness of late blooms. For a while, it felt as if we had found our rhythm again, our family roots finally settling deep into solid ground. I believed the hardest parts were behind us.

But storms never announce themselves with thunder right away. Sometimes they creep in under the warmest skies. Nate's diagnosis came like the first sharp crack, splitting the golden hush wide open. Suddenly, we were scrambling to hold on—to hope, to healing, to the life we had fought so hard to build. We clung desperately to each other, to belief, to love. But exhaustion seeped into the cracks we hadn't seen forming. The foundation we thought had finally set strong beneath us shuddered again, straining under the weight of what we now had to carry. And though we stood together, we could feel it—the ground had shifted beneath our feet.

Chapter 7

Fractured Bloom

A month after his first procedure, I opened my eyes in Nate's hospital room, the cold leather of the recliner chair beneath me, the thin scratchy material of a hospital blanket pulled up under my chin. The window filtered natural light across the glossy white floor, and I wished that we could be at home, enjoying the changing season in our backyard garden where I had begun planting vibrant yellow and orange mums to brighten his days at home.

My attention snapped back to the hospital room. Nate lay in bed next to my chair, asleep. I watched as the peaks and valleys of his heartbeat traveled across the monitor in a familiar pattern. I noticed his chest rise and fall as he slept. I tried to be still and quiet so I didn't wake him or his roommate on the other side of the thin fabric curtain in the center of the room.

It had been a long night as I drifted in and out of sleep between nurse visits to check on his vitals and alarm chimes seeking attention. His new roommate had ordered room service at 10 p.m. the night before and left his lights on and TV on high volume so he could hear it over the breathing devices.

I was exhausted but didn't want to be anywhere else but by Nate's side. He had been in and out of the hospital several times in the last couple months, staying days or weeks at a time, so many times that I had started accidentally calling it a hotel instead of a hospital. It had become our home away from home. Our hospital trips had become so frequent, I kept a packed suitcase and a container of food in the back of my SUV.

Nate's eyes opened and turned his head toward my chair. He smiled as our eyes met. "I'm glad you're here," he whispered. "You're my best therapy."

Wherever he went, I went. I drove him to his appointments, and I spent many nights curled up in the uncomfortable reclining chair next to his hospital bed. Occasionally I would sneak into his hospital bed to gently lie next to him and we would hold each other. I was scared to leave his side, worried that each moment could be our last.

The hospital was about a two-hour drive from our home, so staying at the hospital seemed to be the only option in my mind. I was thankful my mom took good care of the kids for us while we were at the hospital and family members took turns hosting Ruby.

I could hear Nate's roommate shifting around, yelling out for a nurse, his call light beeping. I heard the nurse enter the room and he said, "That *person* used my bathroom."

I cringed.

I knew he was talking about me. I had tried to be quiet when I got up to use the bathroom, not wanting to wake him and wanting to avoid going out into the hall. Sometimes Nate had a room to himself; those were my favorite times. Other times he shared a room, and those times were challenging—for the lack of privacy and because the nights were filled with extra lights and noises.

The nurse suddenly appeared from the other side of the curtain.

"Sorry," she mouthed, her expression sympathetic.

We had already been there for several days this time. I was getting to know the hospital staff and they all seemed fine with me being there, bringing me extra blankets and socks and quickly tracking down a reclining chair if there wasn't one in the room already.

"For now, you can use the staff bathroom down the hall," she said, "and I will bring you some things so you can take a shower down the hall too."

"Thank you so much, I really am sorry." I smiled apologetically, appreciating her kindness at this moment when I really needed it.

I gathered up the tiny shampoo bottle, soap, and towel the nurse had brought me and followed her directions to a supply closet down the hall. A yellow wheeled bucket next to the shower held a mop with its head submerged beneath the dirty brown water, the familiar smell of mop water filling the tiny closet. The shower was not quite hot, but it was refreshing for a moment to just stand there and let the water cascade down my long brown hair and tired, slender body.

My mind wandered. I was tired and wanted life to go back to the way it was before the lies, before the cancer. I didn't sleep much these days, even when we were at home. I lived in a constant state of fear— fear of him dying if I left the room or if I closed my eyes too long. Fear I would drop one of the many tasks, activities, and commitments I was juggling.

Between finding care for the kids and the puppy and working full-time and somehow meeting a self-imposed expectation of maintaining a 4.0 grade point average in my graduate classes, I felt myself pulled in every direction. I attempted to keep the house and yard in order, appeasing the ruthless homeowner's association and maintaining a soothing garden space for Nate to retreat to when he was home.

I was concerned about maintaining a high level of work output working as a training manager, fearful of losing my job because I was now the sole financial support for our family of four and my paychecks were half of what Nate's had been. The costs of oncology visits, treatments, medications, and hospital bills were piling up already, and I spent hours researching and applying for charity programs to cover his expenses.

I had so much to do and think about and remember, the lists would often cycle and loop over and over in my head, as if repeating the lists would help me keep track of everything I was so desperate to remember.

Who else is going to remember if not me? I turned off the water and stood naked, my bare feet on the cement floor of the closet. I shivered as I pulled the thin towel around me and cried.

In that moment, I realized something powerful. In the face of overwhelming responsibilities and uncertainty, I had found a resilience I never knew existed. Every challenge, every sleepless night, every moment of fear had forged a strength within me that would carry me through the uncharted road ahead. Though life had thrown us into chaos, I'd learned that love, even in the hardest moments, was not just about being present but about truly showing up—with kindness, with sacrifice, with an unwavering commitment to hope.

Nate's optimism, his ability to wake up each day and say he was thankful to be alive, his steadfast commitment to "just keep moving" while giving his signature two thumbs-up became a lesson I carried forward. No matter how heavy the burden, I could choose to lift my head, find a moment of joy, and believe that somehow we would find our way through.

In November, the shifting moods of autumn surrendered to the cold, damp grip of winter. Nate and I drove to Seattle for his monthly treatment, the sky heavy with clouds, casting a soft diffused light over the landscape as raindrops began to hit the windshield. I wondered if we would ever have an easy treatment day. His body seemed to reject the treatments that attacked not only the cancer but also the healthy parts of him too.

On this day, he ended up developing sepsis as a result of the treatment, and his organs began to shut down. They rushed him to intensive care and put a breathing tube into his throat.

I wasn't allowed to stay in the ICU room with him, so I ran to the parking garage, splashing through puddles on my way, carrying Nate's bag of personal belongings. I dropped the seats down in the back of my SUV and plugged in his cell phone so it would be charged for when he woke up. I cozied up under my nest of blankets, prepared to take a nap, but I heard the ping of a text alert on Nate's phone before I nodded off.

I lay there a moment and wondered if it was one of his students or his family. I had become the messenger, relaying information in times when Nate couldn't or wouldn't. Sometimes the constant ping of alerts or phone calls would overwhelm me. I touched the button that opened his phone screen and read, "Nate, why aren't you calling me back?" It was Dolores.

I had a sick feeling in my stomach. I scrolled up and saw that she had sent several other texts for him to call her. Since Lilly had come to live with us, Nate had taken more of an active role in facilitating time between Lilly and Dolores. I was thankful since the drama she caused created more stress for me.

I noticed that there was also a voicemail from her. I hadn't heard her voice in a while, and I braced myself as I clicked the play button. "Call me as soon as you get this, Nathan. I need to know what date you want me to fly up there and when you will have our new apartment. I can't wait for us to live together and be a family again."

My heart sank.

What was she talking about? I felt gutted. He was planning to move Dolores back to Washington and get an apartment with her? How long had he been talking to her about moving in together?

We'd had issues in our relationship before he got cancer, and while things between us were better, we still struggled at times. As much as we had tried to heal the fractures in our structure, they were amplified by our exhaustion and anger toward the disease and knowing that the end was coming.

The kids were distressed, medical bills continued to pour in, now approaching the million-dollar mark, and I was hanging on by a thin, frayed thread. It was harder for me to control my meltdowns as I became more and more depressed and overwhelmed.

I opened Dolores's text message and hastily typed, "Leave me alone, I don't want to talk to you anymore." I hovered over the send button, my thumb shaking, before finally clicking send.

The phone rang. It was Dolores.

Scared, I declined the call.

I heard the ping of a new text. "Angie! I know it's you, hahahaha. You must know by now, but you won't keep me away."

I replied, "I don't want anything to do with you."

Ping. "You can't stop us from being together, Angie."

I turned off his cell phone and took a walk around the hospital grounds to calm myself down before returning to the ICU. I clutched his cell phone tightly in one hand, the other hand pressed against my heart, as if it would fall out if I didn't.

I watched Nate sleep; they had kept him unconscious to give him extra time to heal from the sepsis. The nurses told me they were going to wake him, explaining that it could be difficult for him waking up intubated—he wouldn't be able to talk or swallow, and that could be scary for him. I stood next to him as they adjusted his IV fluids and medications. His eyes slowly fluttered and then suddenly shot open. There was a look of horror in his eyes as he realized he couldn't breathe on his own, his body tensed. The nurse explained to him that he was in the hospital and intubated because of the sepsis, but that he had recovered and they would remove the tube shortly.

I stood, holding his hand, gently touching his arm.

"Everything is going to be okay," I reassured him.

His body relaxed. I didn't mention the phone messages. I didn't know what I was going to do yet, but for now, he didn't need that stress.

That night at home, I stepped into the large garden tub in our master bathroom. The hot water ran from the tap, and a large scoop of Epsom salts dissolved at the bottom of the tub. My feet and legs turned red as the water covered my skin and steam rolled off the surface. I leaned back against the hard surface of the tub as I held Nate's phone in my hand. I felt guilty for checking his phone, but neither of us were supposed to have anything to hide. He would often ask me to respond to texts on his phone, to contact people for him or look up information.

I scrolled through the text messages between him and Dolores, then listened to her voicemail again. She had left other messages after I'd shut his phone off earlier. I didn't know what to do; I was maxed out and doing my best, and if he wanted to move in with Dolores, then so be it. I had no more fight left in me.

The next morning, I woke up feeling angry about more lies, more deception—the man who had once been my best friend, the man who I thought I could trust, now felt like a stranger. I packed his things in his car and drove to the hospital. I entered his hospital room where he sat up in bed, alert and smiling, as if nothing were wrong.

I confronted him about the voicemails, the texts, and his plans to get an apartment with Dolores. He was shocked and tried to say Dolores was crazy, but yes, they had discussed the possibility.

"It sounds like she thinks it's a lot more than a possibility," I said as I placed the car key and his phone on his bedside tray. "You need to figure this out."

I wrote down the number of the parking space where I had parked his car, and I left the hospital.

I felt like a horrible person for just leaving him there, but I also felt incredibly hurt and betrayed. I had spent every moment of my days doing everything I could to make sure he was comfortable, cared for, and loved. For what? For him to just leave me? For him to stab me in the back with the woman who had created so much stress for both of us?

Nate stayed with some friends for a couple weeks and then came back home, offering apologies and promises of honesty, of building trust. I didn't know if I could trust him, and I felt a conflict of shame—for abandoning him, and for letting him come back.

He moved himself into the downstairs room that we had used as an office, and he spent all hours of the day and night playing video games and watching movies.

Winter came in cruel, relentless waves, each storm stripping away another layer of what we had built together. It was a season that did not simply arrive; it invaded, seeping into the cracks of our home, our finances, and our resolve. The cold wasn't just outside; it seeped into my bones, in spaces between us where warmth used to be.

The betrayal cut first, swift as an icy wind that steals your breath before you even know you're choking. Then came the weight of too many burdens I'd convinced myself I could carry alone.

But winter doesn't care for resilience. It tests it, bends it, watches to see if it will snap. Mine waivered. I had taken on too much, was stretched too thin across the endless gray, and somewhere in the deep freeze of those months, I felt it: the quiet unraveling of us.

Chapter 8
Silent Thaw

February lingered between worlds. The last grip of winter clung tight even as whispers of warmth stirred beneath the surface. It was a season of quiet hope pressing against the still-frozen ground. In the same way, our hearts, battered and brittle from the seasons we endured, began to thaw too.

That was the month we divorced. Not out of anger, or bitterness, but out of survival. It was a decision born not from the heart but from necessity—a division of assets, a legal reordering meant to protect what little security we had left. On paper, it was practical. Sensible. Heartbreaking.

"If we finalize the divorce," he said quietly, "we can put the important things, like the house, in your name. My debts, my medical bills ... they'll stay with me. At least you won't lose everything."

It was a cold, brutal truth: Cancer wasn't just a thief of time; it was a thief of futures too. The cost of survival wasn't just measured in heartache but in hard, relentless numbers.

On paper, it made sense. But no matter how reasonable it looked in black and white, it didn't feel right. Not to our hearts. Even battered, even fragile, our foundation still pulsed with the life we had built together. It made sense to the outside world, perhaps.

But inside our home, inside our chests, it was a wound that no logic could soothe.

As spring approached, the crocuses emerged from their winter slumber. The tiny buds pushed through the cold, hard ground, the first signs of renewal after the harsh winter. I felt a spark of hope each time I saw a tiny flower tip break through the soil. Each purple petal would push toward the sky and unfold, a promise of warmer days ahead. The crocuses gave me hope that even though we had been through the harshest winter yet, spring would still come.

One afternoon, as the soft light of spring filtered through our bedroom curtains, Nate and I sat on the edge of the bed, facing one another. My body slumped, one leg tucked under me, my hands clenched on my lap, my gaze turned down. He raised his hand and gently touched my chin, nudging me to look at him. His bright blue eyes looked into my soul, searching. He traced the outline of my face, as he had done so many times before, then kissed my nose.

"I've memorized every bit of you," he said softly. "I'll never forget."

His fingers traced the length of my neck and the curve of my shoulder, slowly moving down my arm and gently caressing the back of my hands with his thumbs until I softened. I opened my hands to hold his.

He took a deep breath, then spoke softly. "I love you, sweets. You deserve happiness."

I was trying to be brave and held back the tears that seemed to be a continuous churn behind the cold wall. I had been building a wall inside myself, a dam of resolve designed to hold back the rising tide of sorrow. It stood firm against the pressure, straining to contain the heartbreak threatening to break free. Every unspoken fear, every buried tear pressed harder against it, like floodwaters swelling behind a brittle gate. I knew that if even one crack formed, the entire wall would collapse, and all the grief I had kept contained would come rushing out in a torrent I wasn't sure I could survive. So I braced it, day after day, patching it with silence, with strength, with sheer will.

"Whatever happens," he continued, "I want you to be happy. Find a man who will take care of you the way you deserve. One who will be good to you, kind to you. A man who will love you, cherish you, and be honest with you."

Nate's eyes drilled into the depths of my soul, and I could feel his pain that he would not be part of my future. I knew he was being genuine and selfless.

"You're going to get better," I whispered.

"I will always love you. Death cannot stop true love. All it can do is delay it for a while." He whispered the quote he had recited many times since our first date.

Warm tears ran down my face and he pulled me close. His body was so thin, I could feel his bones.

Later that day, I walked into the master bathroom and my eye caught something on my mirror. Nate had written me a note with a pink paint marker. We had been writing sweet messages to one another on our bathroom mirrors for years. This would be the last mirror message he would write to me. In all capital letters, he had written:

YOU

DESERVE

HAPPINESS

I drew in a slow, heavy breath. The ache in my chest was as constant as the chill in the air. Happiness felt like a distant horizon, barely visible through the lingering weight of winter that refused to loosen its grip. I wondered if I would ever feel light again. And yet, in the quiet, beneath the sorrow, small promises stirred. Whispers of warmer days, new treatments, and the fragile hope of miracles. Like the crocuses pushing bravely through the frozen ground, these tender signs taught me that beauty isn't in endless flowering but in the courage to come back after the fall.

Chapter 9

Last Dance

Spring came, and glimmers of hope gave us determination to enjoy life's small moments together. Life was short, cancer or not, and it had felt heavy for so long. We knew that we needed to get back to what we did best—and that was to live. Beyond the disease and appointments, we tried to capture little moments, going camping and taking road trips. As the chill of winter hung on and spring approached, we drove to the Redwood Forest National Park to sit beneath the towering trees and absorb their healing energy. Spring turned to summer, and we bought a tiny camper so we could travel the coast where Nate could spend short spurts sitting cross-legged on the beach, the waves drowning out any discomfort he might have been feeling. It was his sanctuary, and it gave me hope that life could feel remotely normal once again, our exuberance for adventure and making the most of the limited days we were granted.

During the last days of summer, our weekend adventures and spending quality time together seemed to rekindle the peace between us. I left work early to drive Nate to one of his oncology appointments, and as we sat in the waiting room, I watched as people walked past, some pausing at the lobby coffee stand. The sound of the espresso machine sputtered, the smell of coffee rousing my taste buds.

I looked over at Nate and attempted a tired smile. I moved my hand over his, our fingers locked together. I was worried about having to take another afternoon off work, and at the same time, I was glad that I could still be there for him.

It had been a rough thirteen months since his diagnosis, so many treatments, infections, stent implants, sepsis. The turmoil it caused for each of us, for our relationship, the impact it had on our children, our families, our friends, reached far beyond our tiny pod. On each visit we hoped for good news, that the cancer had slowed down or that the tumors were miraculously smaller, but each time the news was worse, or he would end up in the hospital again.

I wanted us to be at home with our kids and Ruby, kicking back in the backyard under the paper birch tree in the white Adirondack chairs. I longed to dig in the dirt with our hands, planting beans and peas as we had done before in our small backyard garden, to listen to the leaves of the cherry plum trees as the breeze would hit them in the afternoon.

It seemed like he was more comfortable being in the hospital— surrounded by quick medical attention should he need it. I could understand, but I still wished we could be at home.

Nate turned to me and smiled. He stood up next to his chair and extended his other hand toward me, gently pulling me out of my chair.

"What are you doing?" I asked, looking around nervously.

"Dance with me," he replied.

I looked around the waiting room. "There is no music, and there are people," I whispered.

He smiled. "That's okay." He pulled me close and whispered in my ear, "Never stop dancing."

I buried my face in his shoulder, and we slow danced. In that moment, the beautiful memories of moments shared came rushing in and my heart felt soothed as his tired body embraced mine.

The moment was a beautiful testament to the Nate I knew so well in the beginning—his philosophy of life, his way of grasping positive moments of joy, of bringing a smile to my face when I was feeling low. He had lifted me up so many times when I didn't think I was strong enough to endure the hardships. Moments like these, when the whole world disappeared and it was only us, reinforced the why.

Love was our why.

As summer faded to autumn, I prepared at work for a large training event in downtown Seattle. After a year's worth of work planning and coordinating, hundreds of people would arrive at the venue for a three-day lineup of speakers, off-site events, dinners, and receptions. My work schedule was going to be busy, starting early in the morning and ending late at night.

"Can you drop me off at the hospital in Seattle when you go?" Nate asked. "I will meet with my oncologist and see if I can check myself in there."

"If you're sure you won't be more comfortable at home," I said, "I can do that."

It became clear that Nate was anxious about me being so far away in case something went wrong. He hadn't been sleeping much lately, scared that his time was soon. I was scared too. It's a different kind of unsettled feeling when the reality sinks in that we're never guaranteed anything beyond the moment we're in.

I made some last-minute arrangements for my family to pick up Max and feed Ruby while Lilly stayed with friends, then dropped Nate off at the hospital before driving to my hotel.

While I was unpacking my suitcase in my hotel room, my phone rang.

"I'm finished with my doctor, and they won't let me stay at the hospital." Nate's voice sounded defeated.

"Come stay here in my hotel suite!" I told him. "It is a beautiful room with gorgeous views and a giant claw foot tub with doors that open to see the view. I won't be too far if you need me!"

He agreed and took a taxi to the hotel. When he arrived, I eagerly showed him around the suite, excited to make him comfortable and draw him a warm, luxurious bath before I headed out to my first event. He stepped into the deep tub, holding onto the edges as he lowered himself down.

Nate smiled at me as he exhaled and his body softened. "Thank you, this feels good."

"Good." I smiled and kissed his forehead. "I've got to run to the event center to prepare for tomorrow. I love you and will see you in a little bit."

The next morning, I left the room quietly. Nate was still asleep, and I didn't want to disturb him.

At the event center, I checked in with the event staff, making sure that the speakers were on-site and that the registration tables were in place and breakfast and coffee were ready.

I was suddenly nauseous and dizzy; in my gut I felt like something was off. I called Nate, and he didn't answer. *Maybe he's still asleep*, I thought. I talked to the event staff and delegated responsibility to cover me for a little bit so I could go check on Nate. I returned to the room and found him lying on the bed, awake, his back toward me.

"Are you okay?" I asked.

"Yes," he whispered.

I didn't believe him. Something was wrong but he wouldn't talk about it, so I just lay with him and held him as he wept. Suddenly, the nausea I'd felt earlier resurfaced. I rolled off the bed and rushed to the bathroom. I lifted the toilet seat and threw up, my body violently ejecting the yellow bile from my empty stomach. The bitter taste lingered in my mouth as I sat on the bathroom floor.

I looked at the time and took a deep breath. I had been gone for an hour, and I needed to get back to the event.

"I need to get back," I whispered.

"I'm fine, don't worry about me," he insisted.

Torn between staying by his side and the looming feeling that I was already taking too much time off work, I lifted myself off the bathroom floor. I smoothed my hair with my hands, brushed my teeth, wiped the wrinkles out of my skirt, and rushed back. I was intercepted by a manager as I entered the meeting space, who told me that it was unacceptable behavior to leave the event.

Exhausted and overwhelmed by emotion, I didn't know what to do. I was scared to lose my job, and I also felt like a child being scolded.

I seemed to be dropping the ball more and more lately.

I scolded myself. *You should know better, Angie.*

Work was one area where I couldn't afford to mess up. We needed my income.

As autumn deepened and wove its web around us, the crisp, cool air was back. The winds began to howl. I felt the shift of season in my bones, as thick hoodies replaced our summer T-shirts. Nate had retired most of his clothes that hung off his frail frame, hiding his bloated belly beneath oversize hoodies.

"Sweets," Nate said, taking my hand, "I've talked to my family, and they're going to help take care of me so you can have a break. You are doing so much and you're tired all the time."

"I'm okay. I know I'm tired, but I'll do better." My heart sank at the thought of him leaving. He'd been back to Ohio a few times over the last year and a half, and each time I was torn between deep gratitude that he had time to connect and strengthen the bonds with his family and deep despair at the realization that it might be the last time I'd see him.

"There are more of them there, and I'm going to heal and get better. Then I'm going to come back, and we're going to live happily ever after!" he insisted, flashing a smile at me.

I felt guilty for needing a break, but the weight of trying to hold our lives together on top of our relationship struggles was often more than I could manage. I had friends help out now and then, and my family watched the kids and Ruby. Still, I couldn't escape the 24-7 struggle that lived inside my brain with racing thoughts and feeling terrified that he could die any minute.

I felt like I was giving it everything I had, yet it never seemed to be enough. My exhaustion made me emotional, and his exhaustion made him irritated with me for being emotional. This left me apologizing constantly for not doing better, depleting me even more. The truth was the disease had consumed both of us. Each time he left, I still wasn't able to rest. I struggled when he was gone.

It was a clear October evening as we drove to Sea-Tac Airport. When we got there, I told Nate, "I'll park in the garage and walk you to your gate."

"No, just drop me off at the departures curb," he replied, smiling at me tiredly. "I called ahead, and they will have a wheelchair that can take me to the gate."

Hesitantly, I followed the signs for the departure drop-off. I got out of the SUV and opened the back hatch to pull out his suitcase.

I looked at the porter. "Can you make sure he gets his wheelchair to his gate?"

When I turned toward Nate, my heart felt heavy. "I love you," I whispered as he put his arms around me.

"I love you too," he whispered back. "Don't worry, I'll be back and better than ever."

We looked into each other's eyes before parting. *Be strong,* I told myself as I got back into the driver's seat and rolled down the passenger window.

"See you soon," he said with a wave. "I love you!"

I remembered the first time I'd dropped him off at the airport six years earlier. I couldn't wait to get home to book a ticket to go see him.

"See you soon," I said through the open passenger window. "I love you too!" I pulled away from the curb as I watched him disappear through the automatic door and into the airport.

Nate called me when he got to his gate. "They didn't have a wheelchair for me, so I walked."

"What?" I was angry at the airlines and frustrated with myself for not insisting on getting him to his gate.

"I'm pretty exhausted from the walk, so I'll talk to you later, sweets. I'm going to rest."

Once he got to Ohio, I didn't hear from him much and started to worry.

"I'm just giving you some time to rest and not worry about me, sweets," he told me on the phone. "I've been reflecting on how I've blamed myself for not having enough faith to heal myself. I carry that burden about my healing, and it gets me down sometimes."

I tried to reassure him, console him, remind him that he'd been doing his best.

Once upon a time, he had been the most positive person I'd ever met. Sometimes it would annoy me that he was overly positive in situations that didn't deserve positivity. I realized that his irritability and lashing out at me was his anger at the disease, not me. He had been blaming himself for not doing better, for not having the faith to heal himself. We each had our own struggles, and we had a common enemy: cancer.

With him gone, I couldn't rest. I felt distressed and worried. I tried reaching out, missing him and our time together. I just wanted to hear his voice to know that he was okay, but he stopped answering his phone and responding to messages. I was so sick with worry, I called his mom.

"Angie." She paused. "He overdosed on his medications and had to be taken to the hospital."

Overdosed? How could he have overdosed?

"Oh no," I choked out, "is he okay? What happened?"

She responded, "I think he got confused about which medication he was supposed to take and when. They said his liver failed. He is out of the hospital but he's sleeping all the time. His doctor here pulled me aside to let me know that his Seattle doctor told him he only had three months to live. Did you know about this?"

I gasped. "No, I didn't. He didn't say anything to me."

I wondered if he'd found out that day at his appointment in Seattle and didn't tell me. I recalled the nauseous feeling I'd had that something was off, him lying with his back turned to me on the bed in the hotel suite, him crying as I held him, me running to throw up. Or had he known longer than that?

No, he didn't tell me, I thought. *He told me he was going to get better and come back home.* I felt the ground tilt beneath me, as if the earth itself had pulled away. *Three months.* Three months, when I thought we had more summers left.

Grief wrapped itself around my ribs like a vice. I couldn't breathe. I couldn't think. So I did the only thing I knew to do.

I called my dad.

His voice cracked over the line, rough with the memory of losing his second wife to cancer, but it was steady enough to hold me.

"I know," he said. "I know how this feels. I'll be right over."

As we sat on my couch, the silence between us wasn't empty; instead, it was full—full of shared sorrow, of understanding, of the heavy knowledge of what came next. And for the first time that night, wrapped in his strong hug, I didn't feel completely alone.

Chapter 10
Whispering Winds

Outside my office window, the world spun on as if nothing had changed. The dark ominous clouds filled the late October sky, threatening rain. For me, time collapsed into a single, shattering moment. Nate was heavy on my mind.

I swiveled in my desk chair, the ordinary buzz of work humming around me, when my cell phone rang.

It was Nate's brother. "Hey, Angie. It's Jared." There was a long pause. "They don't think Nathan will make it through the weekend."

Jared put Nate on the phone. I strained to hear him; his breath was labored. "I love you, Angie," he softly whispered, as if it were his last breath.

I felt panicked. "I love you too! I'm on my way, I'm coming to you. I will be on the next plane, okay? I'll see you soon!"

Jared and I talked briefly, and I told him I was booking the next flight out. I shuffled a couple things around at work and told my assistant what needed to be done in my absence. I emailed my boss, booked the next flight to Ohio, and called my mom for a ride to the airport.

On my way to the airport, my phone rang. It was my boss. "How dare you leave without giving more notice," she said.

"I explained in my email that Nate is dying and I need to get to him as soon as possible," I said, trying to remain calm.

"You should be responsible enough to finish your workday before leaving," she lectured me.

"But I made sure everything is covered . . ." I gasped as I looked out the car window, my brain racing to process how this could even be an issue. What kind of a person was she? Where was her humanity? I was worried that Nate would die and that I would also lose my job, flunk out of school, fail as a parent to children who were also worried that Nate would die. And now, reality was here. *How dare she lecture me now.*

"We will talk about this when you get back," she said, and hung up.

Getting to Ohio seemed to happen at a snail's pace as traffic crawled slowly along the interstate. I knew security lines at the airport would be painfully long, and I anticipated a two-hour layover in Chicago because there were no direct flights. Now I also had the looming conversation with my boss when I got back. I wondered if I would even have a job after all of this.

"Are you okay?" my mom asked, looking at me with concern from the driver's seat.

"No. I just need to get to him as soon as possible."

On the plane, I watched the screen on the back of the seat in front of me. Outside my window the sky was dark and menacing, and the plane started to shake with turbulence. Hurricane Sandy was thrashing the Northeast with tropical storm forces, and as the plane shook, I felt something else deep within me. I shook my head. *No. No, no, no, no, no!* I held my hand on my heart and closed my eyes. Nate always loved the wind; he said it made him feel so free. It would be like him to hitch a ride on a tropical storm. I'd heard people say that they could feel it when a loved one passed. I felt it, but I just didn't want it to be true.

When I got off the plane in Chicago, I called Jared.

Jared's wife, Arial, answered. "Hey, Angie."

"Hi, Arial. I've landed in Chicago and my next flight is on time. I want to go directly to the hospice center tonight, I don't care how late it is. I will sleep in a chair or on the floor, it doesn't matter—I just want to get to him," I said, not giving pause for bad news that I didn't want to believe.

"Jared is in the other room. I'll have him call you right back, okay?" Arial's voice was soft on the phone.

I sat on a cold leather airport bench seat near my gate, clutching my bag to my chest and holding my phone in my hand as I stared at it. It finally rang.

"Angie, it's Jared. I'm so sorry, I wanted to be the one to tell you: Nathan passed away."

I didn't make it in time. The reality hit me as I looked around me at the people moving so quickly to get to their destinations, my heart shattering into a million tiny pieces. I gasped for air, and the tears flowed. I closed my eyes, wanting to be alone so I could scream and at the same time praying for support, needing comfort. I clutched my bag closer as I hung up the call, my mind reeling. I knew it—the timing matched up with when I'd felt him riding on the wind.

A man paused in front of me, a tender smile on his face. He reached out his hand and gently touched my shoulder. "Bless you," he said. "Everything will be okay." He gave me a reassuring smile as he quickly left.

I felt a moment of warmth from the unexpected kindness and hope in my moment of deep pain, as if my prayer for support and comfort had been delivered.

The next few hours were a blur as I flew the short distance from Chicago to Ohio and somehow ended up at Nate's mom's house. I climbed the stairs to the second-floor guest room and collapsed onto the bed where Nate and I had spent our last night in Ohio before we made the cross-country drive to our new life together in Washington. The very bed where I'd presented him with the scrapbook. We were so excited back then, the adventures we planned to have, the pages in the photo book we would fill. We really did pack so much life into such a short time.

I wept quietly in the dark. My heart ached for those days back, for him to be here with me.

"Nate," I whispered in the dark.

"Angie," I heard my name whispered in return.

I held my breath, silencing the ache for a moment to listen.

I sat up, turned on the lamp, and looked around. I was alone; everyone else had gone to bed. I clicked the lamp off again and laid my head back on the pillow, quietly staring into the darkness and expecting to hear it again. Suddenly, I felt the familiar feeling of Nate's arms wrap around me as I had so many times before. I felt safe and warm, and my body relaxed as I felt love surround me. I drifted into a deep sleep for the first time in as long as I could remember.

I saw him for the last time the next day, although it wasn't really him. My mind was playing tricks on me, not able to grasp that he was gone. I anticipated around every corner that he would pop out and say, "Just kidding!" Perhaps some elaborate scheme to get me here to tell me he really did get better after all.

The funeral director asked if I wanted to go see him. *Go see him?* I'd never seen a dead body before and wasn't sure if I could handle it. But I knew I had to accept that he was really gone so I agreed and went in, the clergyman and Nate's family accompanying me. Nate was wearing a hospital gown and a blanket. His eyes were closed, and he looked like he was sleeping. My hand instinctively extended; I touched his chest, his heart. I expected him to open his eyes, but he felt different, cold, solid. It wasn't him anymore. Thirty-seven years of beautiful life lived in this body, with the last fifteen months in a fight against cancer and the clock. Now, his energy and light were gone—I imagined his spirit catching rides on the winds with childlike glee, soaring above on the wings of a hawk.

As my heart broke open, his family held and comforted me. The clergyman told me to eat and take care of myself and said some kind words. Did he know that I hadn't been eating? My body was distressed and thin; food made me nauseous. I had lost thirty pounds in the last month alone and weighed 120 pounds. My five-foot, ten-inch frame was bony and weak, my collarbone and ribs showing through my skin, my eyes sunken and dark. The cancer took him, and it seemed to want to take me too.

I spent the rest of the day with his family, curled up on his mom's couch. I felt the warm comfort of connection and shared love as we looked at pictures and told stories.

I watched as Jared moved around the house, checking on me, his mom, and others. He offered food, beverages, and support. He went to the store to buy me smoothies, the only thing I could keep down. *He is the glue*, I thought. *He is holding us all together.*

A couple of days later, I stood in the hallway of one of the oldest churches in his hometown. Hundreds of people wrapped around the block, waiting to enter the stone church with its arched windows and tall tower. As each person entered the lobby, they approached the line of Nate's parents, siblings, relatives, and me to offer their sympathy. At past events, Nate would have been by my side. He was the social butterfly, the life of the party with his big bellowing laugh and kind eyes. He had that aura that people wanted to be around. At those events, I would safely hide at his side, letting him enjoy the spotlight.

He would try to call attention to me, and I would take a step back, shy and quiet. He'd draw me out and introduce me with a dazzling smile, "And this is my beautiful wife!" Sometimes when I was wearing high heels next to his five-foot-seven stature, he would proudly put his hand on the small of my back and introduce me as his "smokin' hot supermodel wife."

I would blush and redirect the attention back to him. Now, my thin, exhausted body stood there in a borrowed black dress and pearls, with nowhere to hide. I no longer had control of the tears that fell, and I wished more than anything that he could be there by my side to hold me up. I wished that I could stop crying uncontrollably and pull myself together. With each hand of sympathy that extended to touch mine, I whispered thank you as the tears flowed down my cheeks and neck.

The same clergyman from the funeral home delivered the eulogy. He talked of Nate's family, his work, his passions. Most of all, he spoke of how much of an inspiration he was to every life that he touched. The man recalled how even in Nate's final breaths in hospice he was so kind and thankful to the people who were taking care of him. He spoke of the time in the doctor's office when he took my hand and asked me to dance, how he whispered to me to *never stop dancing*. It was a testament to how Nate lived his life.

He wasn't perfect, as none of us are. But he did his best to look for the good in life, to treat others with kindness and find joy in the small things. He was only thirty-seven years old, but he'd lived so fully in the time he had.

Grief struck like the first cruel winds of winter, hollowing out the warmth we had built together. I remembered how on the plane, as Hurricane Sandy thrashed the sky and my heart broke open mid-flight, I knew he had found the wind. I thought of his laughter on breezy days, the way he tilted his face to the sky like he could drink it in. He always said the wind made him feel free. Maybe, in the end, that's exactly where he went. He was free—carried beyond my reach but still in my heart.

In the silence that followed, I wondered if I could survive the storm of his absence. But even in the deepest ache, life whispered. Gentle. Insistent. A reminder that love had existed. That laughter had filled our walls. That every breath, every fragile fleeting moment, was a gift.

And somehow I knew. In honoring the wild, beautiful life we'd built together as fleeting as a gust of wind, I would find a way to keep going.

Chapter 11
First Glimmer

Winter had swallowed the world in its quiet, heavy stillness, and I let it swallow me too. Two months after Nate passed, I cocooned myself in a white queen-size down comforter, my own hibernation from the winter of my life.

As much support as I had from friends and family, it never filled the deep cavern that was left in me. I struggled for relief from the deep grief that he was gone, along with self-loathing, wishing I had done better. For him. For us.

Each night I lay in bed, whispering as tears streamed down my face, "Nate, are you here?" I tried to quiet my heartbeat, hoping to hear a response. Instead, there was silence.

Each morning, I would reluctantly climb out of bed and stare at my bathroom mirror, reading aloud the message that Nate had written: "You deserve happiness!" I would carefully clean the toothpaste smudges from the mirror with my fingertip, scared to disturb the handwritten message.

I felt so broken. I was a zombie at work; I noticed people dodge me in the halls. Max spent more time in his room, trying to fill his time watching funny videos and playing games with his friends, and was missing more school. Lilly went to go live with her mom; our children grieved the loss too.

I worked with my therapist on managing my grief, scared that it would consume me—and Max too.

I didn't realize it back then, but I had been grieving since the day he was diagnosed, and now, my life as I knew it had changed. Shared dreams crumbled around me, days of my life spent worrying, sleeping in the chair alongside his hospital bed, gone. I knew that I had to pick all my broken pieces up and put them back together. For me. For Max. I just didn't know how.

Outside, bare trees stood like skeletons against the ashen sky, the air sharp with the bite of December. Inside, I drowned out the silence with the flickering glow of the television, the sweet warmth of my snuggle companion, Ruby, nestled against me.

My phone chirped. It was a text from my friend Nala.

"What are you doing?" she asked.

"Lying on the couch. Wallowing," I replied honestly.

"Get off the couch and do something," she insisted.

I could imagine her face if she were there in person, her lips pursed in a bossy yet teasing way, the large curls of her shoulder-length pink hair bouncing as she shook her head at me. Her grass-green Mary Janes would tap on the ground, and then she'd surely flash me a smile. She was always the friend who showed up, who made sure everyone was fed with her delicious home cooking and that everyone felt loved.

I protested, "No, I have no local friends, and I don't want to go anywhere alone."

Nate had become the central part of my life for over six years, our constant adventures and explorations, the long cancer journey that consumed both of us. Even before Nate, I had gone from home, to college, to married, to divorced and adventuring in video games from the safety of my house. I had never been good at doing things alone, developing a fear early on that the worst things would happen to me if I was alone.

"You should join Meetup," Nala texted back.

I quickly retorted, "I am not ready to date!" I felt a knot in my stomach at just the thought of dating so soon.

"It's not a dating site," she replied. "It's just a bunch of people who create interest groups, and you go and do things with other people who also don't want to do things alone. Just like you. And it's free to join."

"Oh! That sounds interesting," I replied, curious if there were really others who wanted to do the same things.

I immediately downloaded the app and created an account. I dragged my finger over the phone screen and watched the list of activities appear and disappear as I scrolled. I felt a tiny spark of anticipation as I saw an upcoming event for a winter bus trip to Leavenworth for their annual Christmas Lighting Festival. I had so many great memories of this little Bavarian village in the mountains—family vacations when my son was little, playing in the snow, browsing the charming little shops, enjoying horse-drawn sleigh rides, and eating roasted chestnuts in the snow as the village was lit up with Christmas lights and the song of carolers. The idea of going to a familiar place that I loved sounded like a good plan for adventure.

My finger hovered over the "Confirm Payment" button. If I went, I could end up sitting alone in a town full of happy strangers, my loneliness amplified under the twinkle of Christmas lights. But if I didn't go, I already knew what would happen: I would stay here, wrapped in my comforter, watching other people live their lives on a screen. I swallowed hard, and clicked. The confirmation screen flashed, and my stomach twisted with regret and excitement in equal measure.

The next weekend, I drove to the park and ride for my first Meetup event. I waited near the long tour bus, looking down at my old pair of winter boots as I stood on the sidewalk. I felt self-conscious and shy, wondering if I should have bought some new boots, wanting to fit in. I watched as people greeted each other with recognition and enthusiastic smiles.

A few people approached me. "You must be new here?" they asked and then introduced themselves as I shuffled my feet and picked at my fingers before they drifted off to greet others.

Boarding the bus, I held my breath. The eyes of sixty strangers stared at me as I walked past full rows to an empty seat near the back of the bus, next to another woman.

"Is this seat open?" I asked.

She nodded and shifted in her seat, and we exchanged quick smiles as I settled in. The loud buzz of conversations and laughter surrounded us. I looked around, hopeful that future friends were on that bus who would be a part of this new chapter of my life. Two women sat across the aisle from me, pulling a bottle of champagne out of a soft cooler and filling their glasses as they laughed.

As the bus began to drive away from the park and ride and the roar of greetings softened, I introduced myself to the woman next to me. "Hi! I'm Angie." I smiled.

She used her fingers, forming shapes and gestures. I recognized the sign language as I watched the familiar patterns, but it had been a long time since I'd used sign language, and my understanding was very limited.

Our conversation was brief before she turned and continued to look out the window for the rest of the trip. I thought about my limited sign language knowledge and wished I knew more. I wondered if she felt as alone as I did, but I didn't know how to ask her.

The bus rumbled forward, carrying sixty strangers toward a Christmas town full of memories that didn't include me anymore. Around me, laughter burst like fireworks, contagious and easy, while Jell-O shots and champagne flowed freely. The air buzzed with the scent of liquor and holiday cheer, but I felt like a guest at the party I hadn't been invited to. I had forgotten what it felt like to laugh like that, to be weightless. Would I feel less alone if I joined them? Would alcohol make the ache in my chest more bearable? Or worse?

I started to panic as we approached town, the reality sinking in that I did not know any of these people and I was stuck, headed to a magical Christmas town in the mountains where I would likely still feel alone and broken. I quickly befriended the women across the aisle from me and they offered me a mimosa. I asked them if I could tag along with them for lunch as we pulled into the bus parking lot.

I followed them to a local restaurant, where I had German sausage and sauerkraut with a pint of beer. We wandered in and out of the tiny, crowded village shops that I had been to a dozen times before with my family. I kept the ladies in my sights, fearful of losing them. Snow crunching under my boots, I put my gloved hands in my pockets, the cold air stinging my face.

As we wandered, popping in and out of shops, we talked about the town and the little treasures we found on the shelves.

"Are you married? Dating? Single?" one of the ladies asked me.

I was not prepared for this question. My chest felt heavy and breathing became difficult. What would normally be a simple question suddenly made me feel overwhelmed. How should I respond? My mind raced. I had this overpowering nauseous feeling in my stomach about lying. I couldn't tell a lie. I had to be honest.

A lump formed in my throat as my voice cracked. "I *was* married, and he passed away." I looked down at my tattered boots and noticed a drain in the street. I just wanted to slip down into that hole and disappear.

I was fighting back tears as the questions got harder. "How did he die? What kind of cancer? How long was he sick? When was it?"

I answered their questions as quickly as I could, as I felt the floodgates threaten to release the tears that never stop.

The women looked shocked that it had only been two months ago and patted me sympathetically on the shoulder. I quickly changed the subject, pushing the lump from my throat with a hot mulled wine and a wave of my hand, as if to say, *It's okay.*

But it wasn't okay.

As the sky grew dark in the valley, people gathered in the middle of the snowy streets for the countdown. When it was time, I watched as the lighting of the trees and buildings sent a magical glow into the sky. Thousands of people packed around me, singing carols in the street as fireworks popped and crackled in a colorful display of celebration against the snowcapped mountain backdrop. My heart ached inside my chest, and my eyes scanned the crowd for comfort to no avail—I felt utterly alone.

Memories flooded my mind and heart of standing in that very place years before with Nate and Max, sharing hot chestnuts and hot chocolate, singing, rejoicing in the glow of the lights. I wished Nate and Max were both there with me.

After the lighting, I quietly followed my new friends back to the bus, the glow of the Christmas lights fading as we moved further from the center of town. I climbed the steps and returned to my seat near the back. As the bus pulled out of the lot and the interior lights were turned out, I put my hood over my head in the dark and wept quietly all the way home, hoping that no one would notice.

At home, I stared at my reflection through the pink writing on my bathroom mirror as I rubbed my red, puffy eyes. Tucking my long bangs behind my ear, I lifted my chin and took a deep breath, inhaling the faint smell of the red alstroemeria flowers in the white milk glass vase on the counter. I touched the edge of a petal. I always liked how resilient the alstroemeria were, outlasting every other cut flower I brought home from the grocery store. I knew that I was doing my best, yet sometimes resilience felt fleeting. It had been a difficult day, but I had tried, and I'd survived. Sometimes that first step was the hardest, and maybe next time I could step a bit more slowly, and not so far from home.

As winter turned to spring, I continued to explore the Meetup app. I joined a photography group that met once a month to share our photos and receive feedback. Between meetings, I felt a fire spark inside me as I pulled out the DSLR camera with the macro lens Nate had bought me and studied the world around me up close: ladybugs crawling up a blade of grass, the golden dusting of pollen on the petals and stigma of an open tulip, tiny dewdrop orbs clinging to woodland moss, and the orange sori spores on the back side of a sword fern.

As spring progressed, I spent less time in my blanket burrito and more time in my yard with my camera pressed to my face. Noticing.

I also started noticing that I craved deeper connections with people outside the safety of the tall cedar fence that surrounded the two-story house that had once been filled with laughter, conversations, and love.

As the weather warmed and tiny blossoms started to appear like pieces of pink popcorn on my cherry plum trees, I had a yearning to explore beyond the yard again, to be in nature, my feet on a winding trail up a mountain, soaking in the sights and smells and sounds. The Meetup app offered many hiking groups, and I began scanning them daily as new hikes appeared.

My earliest memory of hiking was climbing a mountain with my dad when I was five years old. I wore my straight, long dark brown hair loose and cascading over my heavy coat, my short legs protected from the elements by dark blue corduroy pants. As we navigated to the top of the mountain, we were above the clouds. Cold, heavy fog and patches of snow surrounded us, the air crisp and still. I felt a chill as we sat down near some trees.

My dad would have been around twenty-two years old at the time. He carried a heavy pack on his six-foot frame, his brown hair curled gently at the ends, a beard and mustache framing his joyful smile and kind blue eyes. He pulled two plastic-wrapped bologna sandwiches from his pack, handing me one. The white bread stuck to the roof of my mouth as the bologna and processed cheese slice mixed with the mayonnaise while I chewed. I shivered as my dad pulled out a tall green thermos.

"Is that cocoa?" I asked.

"It's coffee," he replied with a smile.

He poured the creamy beige liquid into the cap of the thermos, the steam carrying the sweet aroma of cream and sugar toward me.

"Can I have some?" I asked, shivering from the cold.

He hesitated, then offered his cup. I blew on the top of the steaming liquid and took a careful sip. I was anticipating the flavor to be like cocoa, but it wasn't, though it was sweet and creamy. I felt like a grown-up, and enjoyed the special moment shared with my dad.

Most of my childhood was spent adventuring in the mountains and forests—hiking, camping, exploring. As an adult, hiking had become less frequent. Nate and I had hiked several times over the years, and I had gone with friends, but I wanted more of these moments.

As my grief ebbed and flowed, my ability to commit was inconsistent, but I listened to my body and what I needed day by day.

When the spring blooms opened fully, exposing the rainbow of colors in my yard and beyond, my feet hit the trail in a line of strangers. I watched as tiny green sprouts pushed through the cool soil, extending toward the sky, and unfolding delicate blooms.

I noticed the vibrant green tips of new growth on the evergreen trees along the trails, extending my hand to feel the softness with my fingertips as I breathed in the fresh smell of pine. I listened for birdsong and the faint sound of water in the distance between the cadence of trail chatter that ranged from surprised exclamations of nature discoveries to elaborate descriptions of the burgers or tacos we wanted to feast on after the hike.

It felt like just yesterday that grief had settled over me like an endless winter, filling every hollow space Nate's absence left behind. I searched outside myself for anything that might soften the ache, some hint of normalcy, some distraction to anchor me when the ground beneath my feet felt so uncertain. Every step forward felt unsteady, like walking a frozen river whose surface could crack without warning. The weight of sorrow pressed heavy on my shoulders, and still, I pushed myself. Even when I wasn't ready. I climbed mountains when my heart begged me to stay low, testing the limits of my strength in a world that no longer felt familiar.

And yet, somewhere in that fragile discomfort, change began to stir. Quiet at first, like the first breath of spring after a long, bitter freeze. Tiny glimmers. Sunlight lingering a little longer in the sky. The delicate promise of green threading through the thawing earth began to break through the heavy gray. Little by little, life whispered its way back into my bones. The ache was still there, but so, too, was a stirring. A soft excitement for simple things. A hope that maybe, just maybe, I could find joy again in the world that Nate had once loved so deeply.

Chapter 12
Wild Awakening

As spring turned to summer, the full leaves of the deciduous trees rustled in the gentle breeze among the ever-present evergreens. The blue of the sky deepened, and the hills got steeper as higher elevation snows melted, exposing meadows of wildflowers that rekindled the joy of childhood and the excitement of summer adventures.

With each hike, I felt more comfortable, more confident, more connected. Many of the same faces showed up at the trailheads, my worries of the unknown soothed. With each step and each mile, connections deepened with a handful of friends who loved the outdoors and nature as much as I did. I began to feel safe sharing my story authentically and listened to the stories of others, finding intersections in our stories of love, loss, grief, and joy.

That summer was a catalyst that planted tiny seeds of hope that life beyond the grief was possible. It showed me that while the shared dreams would never be, I was still here, and just as Nate never saw his end coming so soon, the reality is that none of us know when our last breath will be.

I lived in duality. I still missed Nate, and I also had pockets of joy. I was viewing the world through new eyes. Eyes that knew how precious life was. Eyes that wanted to capture every color, texture, and pattern and store it away as if it were the first time, as if it were the last time.

One evening in November, with the energizing hikes of summer behind me, I sat at a table in a beautiful waterfront restaurant with a group of friends I'd met hiking. The large wall of windows that overlooked the water were as dark as the night sky and reflected the soft light within the restaurant. It was Hanna's birthday, and I watched as she threw her head back, her thick, long blonde hair flowing down her back as her broad shoulders shook with a big laugh. I smiled, thankful to be invited out and to be with new friends.

It had been a busy thirteen months since Nate had passed and eleven months since I took that first bus ride. I started to get more excited about going out, feeling like I had more local community around me. I had just given notice at the job I had for over seven years and eagerly anticipated a new job writing that felt promising. I was excited for the possibilities that were unfolding.

As I finished my blackened salmon and wild rice pilaf, Hanna said, "What else should we do? Maybe we could go to a bar or go dancing?"

"I know a place," I responded. "There is a country bar downtown that I've been to a couple times in the past that has dancing. It might be fun to try it out."

Heads nodded around the table. "Okay, let's go!"

We pulled our cars into the parking lot of the country bar and headed for the front door, listening to the thump of the music from inside. There was a line, and a bouncer checked IDs while a cashier took our entry fee and stamped the back of our hands. We quickly made our way to the bar for some liquid courage, then continued to the edge of the polished hardwood dance floor to watch the dancers move in sync to the music as we sipped our drinks. I looked on as dancers stomped, kicked, and shuffled in their cowboy boots, their hips shaking in blue jeans, dresses twirling, hats tipping. I could feel the buzz of the alcohol in my blood, and the bass from the speakers thumped inside my body. I wanted to be out on the dance floor too; my lips stretched into a grin as my body started to sway and my toes tapped. I blushed each time I was asked to dance.

Between the occasional two-step with men wearing cowboy hats and boots, I stood at the edge of the dance floor. I watched as others eagerly entered the dance floor, moving in carefully choreographed line dance patterns to music that was foreign to me.

"I would love to learn to dance like that!" I said to a woman next to me.

She smiled and responded, "They have free line dance lessons three nights a week. You should check those out!"

I turned to Hanna with a big smile and eagerly rubbed my hands together. "Want to come back and take lessons? We should! It would be so fun!" I exclaimed, jumping up and down like a child.

"Sounds fun!" she responded as her gaze focused on the dancers twirling in front of her.

I loved the idea of learning the dances, of feeling energized again by music, of having something to look forward to.

"Okay, so we need to go buy some cowboy boots. You know, workout shoes for our workout class." I motioned to the dance floor and shimmied my hips and shoulders back and forth.

Hanna laughed. "Yes, we do!"

A few weeks later, on a Thursday night, Hanna and I arrived together at the country dance bar. I could feel the hug of my brand-new leather cowboy boots on my feet and ankles as we presented our wrists inside the door to get our entry stamp.

"Ready for our workout class?" I teased, clutching my hands together under my chin, my shoulders drawn toward my ears.

I anticipated the lesson as I stood at the wood-wrapped bar, tipping back a shot glass of Knob Creek whiskey. I felt the burn as it hit my throat and moved to my chest. I winced and furrowed my brow, then stuck my tongue out.

"Ahhhh," I said with a cough, "hits the spot."

I laughed and moved to the dance floor as they announced that the lesson was about to start. We stood at the back near the camo-covered barstools and a ledge that separated the bar area from the dance floor. A low red light cascaded across the hardwood floor. Thick, heavy rope draped between posts near large whiskey barrels and a wall of license plates. With the warmth of the whiskey in my chest and belly, my head quickly started to buzz, and the tip of my nose tingled. As the lesson began, I attempted to follow the steps called out, my two left feet fumbling beneath me. It was hard to focus, and I questioned the whiskey shot as the lesson ended and the dance moves quickly faded from my mind.

As weeks turned into months, three lessons a week formed muscle memory in my feet and legs, and I could quickly identify songs and my feet would follow. What had started out a shy arrival with Hanna along for moral support became arriving on my own to the familiar faces of other regulars, many becoming close friends.

Each song was a three-and-a-half-minute opportunity that encouraged me to be fully present in the moment—to stop overthinking, a frequent activity for me off the dance floor. The line dances forced me to be fully emersed in the present moment, each choreographed movement creating muscle memory. I didn't feel like I had to do it perfectly, but I also needed to not overthink, which often caused awkward flailing movements. With line dancing, I followed a pattern, a routine, and I did my best to go with the flow and eventually spin enough times that I would end up facing the same wall as the other dancers on the floor. I disregarded perfection but embraced fun and playfulness. I stopped caring what other people thought, twirling around in my own blissful bubble.

At first, I'd treated two-stepping like a puzzle to be solved, trying to anticipate each move before it happened. But dance doesn't work like that—just like life, it's about trust, being present, and paying attention. I stepped when I shouldn't, leaned the wrong way, apologized a hundred times for misplaced feet. My partners laughed, patient, guiding me through each misstep.

Slowly, I learned to surrender to the rhythm, to feel the slight pressure of a hand on my back, to watch for my partner's hand to open, close, extend, or raise, providing clues on what to expect next. And for the first time, I wasn't overthinking; I was just moving, twirling, existing in the moment.

That summer had a different kind of warmth. Each hike I took, each mountain I climbed, stitched me a little more firmly into the world again. I moved with more confidence, more ease, feeling my body and spirit reconnect after so long adrift. It was on those winding trails, under endless blue skies, that tiny seeds of hope were planted deep inside me.

Grief still traveled with me, a constant shadow, but it no longer consumed all the light. Joy flickered beside it, small at first, then stronger, more insistent. I began to understand that life wasn't meant to be lived in either sorrow or happiness alone; it was a wild, breathtaking mix of both. The more I leaned into that duality, the more precious each moment became.

I danced, laughed until my chest ached, let the simple beauty of being alive burn through me. What had once been a fragile glimmer had now caught fire, a fierce and living flame. For the first time in a long while, I wasn't just surviving; I was existing fully, freely, alive to it all.

Chapter 13
Brave Becoming

Winter passed differently this time, not in stillness but in motion.
I danced through the heavy days, spun my way through grief and
fleeting joy, willing my body to remember what it felt like to be alive,
even when my heart was slow to follow. By the time spring unfurled
its first tender leaves, I found myself sitting in my therapist, Shirley's
office, the bright afternoon light slanting through the window,
carrying more questions than answers.

I leaned forward on the light blue couch and extended my hand
to the crystal candy dish on the small dark brown coffee table. I
selected a red foil-wrapped chocolate square and carefully peeled the
foil out from the center, breathing in the scent of dark chocolate. *My
favorite,* I thought as I placed the chocolate on my tongue.

"I needed this," I said, pointing toward my mouth.

"What's going on?" Shirley tilted her head to the side as she
wrote something on her yellow notepad.

I was curious what she wrote on that yellow notepad. It was
always perched on her lap and occasionally her pen would scroll
across the page. I sometimes imagined she was just drawing pictures
or pretending to write something interesting because she was so
bored with my talking.

Taking a deep breath, I felt the chocolate dissolve in my mouth, and I started to cry. "I'm just feeling so overwhelmed," I began. "I just keep waiting for life to feel normal again."

"Have you considered that you might need a new normal?" Shirley asked, handing me the box of tissues.

"What do you mean?" I said, pulling three tissues from the box and pressing them to my face.

"Well, life won't ever go back to the way it was. Normal for you has changed. You are finding new experiences and living life in new ways. What do you want your new normal to look like?" She smiled at me from her chair, her legs crossed, the yellow notepad balanced on her lap.

"Hmmm," I said, my gaze drifting again to the window as my fingertips twisted the used tissues.

I watched the leaves move lightly in the breeze and noticed some fluffy white clouds slowly glide past. I hadn't thought about how life would never go back to the way it was. I had been searching for feelings and ways of life that were like they were before. I was going through the motions with some things, and finding a lot of joy in others.

I thought about what my new normal looked like. I thought about the dancing, the deep belly laughs. I thought about the hiking I had done last summer, even into the fall and winter. I liked how those things made me feel. I also realized that I had been in a constant longing for the normal that was no longer available to me. I hadn't thought about needing to create a new normal.

"I want to say yes to more things that create joy and happiness in my life and say no to things that take my light." I held my finger up and smiled for the first time. "I also want to sleep!"

"Tell me about your sleep lately." I could hear the question in her tone.

My answer was the same as every other time she asked. Sleep was elusive. I had been seeing a naturopath and was diagnosed with adrenal fatigue and insomnia. The chronic stress of years of hypervigilance to Nate's illness and everything going on in my life had caused adrenal insufficiencies. I was so exhausted, I often fell asleep as soon as my head hit the pillow, but I would wake up every fifteen to thirty minutes throughout the night, my heart racing and my mind whirling with panic and fear, my stomach filled with bubbling gas.

I walked through each day exhausted.

Her pen scrolled across the paper. "I know sleep has been an ongoing concern, and I'm hoping that we can get you sleeping again. Maybe until our next session you can focus on something else. What do you want to focus on until then?"

I sat with her question, the words settling into the quiet spaces of my mind. *A new normal.* I had spent so much time longing for the life I lost, waiting for things to feel the way they used to. I swallowed hard and nodded. "I don't know what my new normal looks like yet . . . but I think it includes hiking. And dancing. And saying yes to things that make me feel alive again."

She put down her pen and placed her notepad on her desk behind her and stood. "Okay, that sounds great. Your homework until next time is to do more things that make you feel good," she said with a smile. "See you in a couple weeks."

As I stood, she gave me a hug.

"See you in a couple weeks," I repeated.

On my drive home, I reflected inward on creating a new normal. I had been trying to figure out what I enjoyed since Nate passed away. I had joined some groups and had been finding joy. I wondered if I could branch out from that to discover even more things that brought me happiness.

I used to love writing. I had been writing for as long as I could remember, even winning first place at a young authors contest when I was in the fourth grade. I had started many novels throughout my teen years, written a stack of children's books, and even self-published a local travel book I'd written before Nate and I met.

I wondered if there was a way to combine fun experiences with my writing.

Suddenly, as if a light bulb had gone off in my head, my body began to buzz with excitement, a new challenge. The light bulb became a neon sign, flashing FORTY-FIVE DAYS OF ADVENTURE!

I smiled. I loved when these light bulb moments happened, as if just by asking for an idea, it suddenly appeared for me to choose it, or not.

The ideas swirled in my head. I could explore more new adventures, and I could develop a new habit of writing daily. I had read something about how forty-five consecutive days of doing something could create new habits. This sounded like a great way to make some new memories and establish a new normal.

For the next forty-five days, I started to live intentionally to feel inspired and joyful. I thought a lot about the value of life and how it really becomes clear once you lose someone close to you how precious our time really is. I looked at the way that life was lived and all the *coulda, woulda, shouldas* did not seem as important as the moments that were fully lived, and the memories made in the process.

The first few days felt clumsy, like trying to walk on legs I hadn't yet grown into. Every new experience tugged at the parts of me that still ached for what was lost. Some days I felt brave, electric with possibility, and other days the weight of starting over pressed so heavily on my chest that even the smallest steps felt impossible.

I kept moving.

I kept saying yes.

A first tattoo. Unlikely adventures. Traveling to new places. Dancing like no one was watching. Each moment a seed, planted not because I was sure it would bloom but because I needed to believe it could.

Somewhere in the messy, uncertain beginning, I started to feel it: not a return to the old me but the tender shaping of someone new. A version of myself shaped by loss, yes, but also resilience, curiosity, and the fierce hope that life, even after so much unraveling, still held beautiful things waiting for me to find them.

The perspective shift happened when I started to view the ordinary things in life in an extraordinary way. When I started to view activities in life (big and small) as adventure, it changed everything. At the end of the forty-five days, I reflected on how much I had grown through the experience, by saying yes to life, and in my writing.

Surprisingly, the ultimate lesson I learned was about self-care. In the process of creating a new normal, I had to establish a new normal of self-care. I discovered that I had to listen to what my body needed, because when I listened, I created space for healing.

I took time to pause after my forty-five days to reboot, to honor that none of us are meant to live with packed calendars and activities every day. Life is short, and my appetite is intense when it comes to wanting to soak up every drop of life, but it is in the quiet moments of rest, meditation, reflection, and gratitude that the magic of those lived experiences are rooted.

The result was that I started to love myself as the individual me rather than the me that had been part of a pair. I started to feel more accepting of my faults, flaws, and imperfections. I started to validate my own worthiness rather than seeking out validation from someone else to confirm that I was enough.

I realized I had been chasing ghosts, trying to recapture a life that no longer existed, clinging to the memory of a normal that had slipped away. The weight of it pressed down harder with every step, until it became clear: I wasn't meant to go back. I was meant to create something new, even if I didn't yet know what that would look like. I knew I couldn't stand still. After forty-five days of saying yes to life, stepping outside the familiar, stretching beyond what I thought I knew, I began the slow, uncertain work of building a new normal— one breath, one brave choice at a time.

Chapter 14
Windswept Farewell

Like the restless winds before a storm, anxiety had always swirled within me, but I never saw it for what it was—continuous gusts of unease that I assumed were normal. Then, sitting in Shirley's office, she named it: generalized anxiety disorder. The words settled over me, a quiet revelation that explained so much: the racing heart, the breathless worry, the endless loop of what-ifs in my mind.

Realizing this was not just fleeting nervousness but a constant undercurrent changed everything. I began recognizing the difference between real threats and the ones my mind created. I learned to pause, to question: Is this true, or is this just the storm of anxiety whispering lies?

For years, Nate had been my shelter from these storms, his presence a grounding force against my inner turbulence. Without him, I had to learn how to calm the winds on my own.

As winter arrived again outside, the turbulence inside me grew. The rains began, unrelenting, the sky a permanent shade of sorrow. That was when Shirley told me she was leaving.

Her words hit like the first freeze of the season. My last tether to Nate, gone. My chest tightened and my breath became shallow, a familiar storm brewing inside me. How could I navigate this grief alone?

Without her, I leaned on Hanna, a steady presence until she, too, withdrew like the fading early light of the day.

"I just can't be your friend anymore," she said.

I wondered what I did wrong. From deep inside my core, I knew. I was the problem. One day, she was there; the next, she wasn't. And just like that, I was left in winter's grip.

My mind spiraled, convincing me I was too much, too broken. Every word I spoke felt like frostbite; every interaction was laced with self-doubt. Anxiety told me I was a burden; grief told me I was alone.

A quiet whisper echoed in my heart. *Everyone leaves.*

The season stretched endlessly, but somewhere deep inside, a quiet truth remained: Winter is not forever.

November arrived with the weight of endings. The trees stood bare, their branches outstretched like open hands surrendering to the sky. The air carried a sharpness, a quiet urgency that whispered, "It's time."

For two years, Nate's ashes had moved from room to room, like the fallen leaves carried by the wind, never settling. The idea of spreading them had felt impossible, like releasing the last piece of him. Every season had passed without the right moment—until now. Winter had always been the hardest, but maybe, like the trees, I had to let go to make space for something new.

The ocean called, and I answered.

The ocean. The ocean had been calling to his soul long before we knew each other. Before we met in person, he would talk about his love for the ocean, and on his first trip to Washington he dipped his toes into the cold Pacific Ocean for the first time. He'd sit on the beach for hours, his legs crossed under him, breathing in the ocean air. We would dream together about where we would like to live . . . someday.

"The ocean!" he'd exclaim, batting his long lashes at me, his blue eyes twinkling with mischievous vigor.

"Lake in the mountains!" I would counter with my own enthusiastic reply, tilting my head to the side, batting my own lashes.

I loved the quiet stillness of the alpine lakes; he loved the roar of the ocean and the wind blowing in his face. We could have been happy in either place together, but his passion for the ocean ran deep. We spent quite a bit of time on our adventures traveling the West Coast collecting trinkets for our beach-themed home. We talked about buying a house on the coast someday in a cute little community where we could display our trinkets, where he could have his personal training studio and I could write books and create art.

That November morning, I made the drive alone. Our dreams would never be a reality together, but I could at least give him his. The weather matched my heavy mood, rainy and cold. Driving alone elevated my anxiety, and it was a long drive, but I knew it was time.

Two hours later, I turned the steering wheel to the left as I parked between the white lines and turned off the engine. I pulled the keys from the ignition and took a deep breath, wondering if I was doing the right thing. I looked around. The parking lot was empty, so I stepped outside as the rain pelted me in the face.

I hesitated a moment before zipping up my turquoise raincoat and pulling a backpack over one shoulder with the small box inside. I took another deep breath and walked toward the sound of crashing waves. As my feet reached the sand, the wind pushed against me like strong hands. I tucked my chin down and leaned forward into the wind; with each step, the wind pushed harder. My feet became heavy with the weight of the task combined with the deep wet sand beneath me. Each step became increasingly difficult. Was my determination being tested or was something saying no, not yet? I fought the wind all the way to the ocean, the waves breaking in an angry roar, and approached the dark jagged rock we had sat on together so many times before.

It was our beach.

It was his beach. I felt him there.

I felt like I was at the final scene of the quest to battle the epic dragon beyond a series of caves, our last quest together. I screamed into the ocean as it kicked up giant waves and sprayed into the sky. The wind threw salty mist across my face.

I sobbed.

I watched the waves crash against the rock. I wondered if the raging ocean was forceful enough to consume me as the grief had and took a step back, suddenly aware of how powerful the ocean was.

I just needed to say goodbye. I needed him to know that I was going to be okay and that I was ready to heal. As much as he had been my entire world for our short time together, it was time for him to know that he didn't need to hold me up anymore. I had to be strong enough to hold myself up now.

The memories came flooding in with each wave: the Valentine's Day weekend when he'd brought me there just so I could use my new camera, the sunrises and sunsets, building sandcastles and flying kites, bringing our kids and our friends there. I looked at the rock next to me and remembered the photograph I'd taken of him with his two thumbs pointed up, sunglasses on, his smile wide. He loved it there.

Shaken by a burst of wind that pushed against my body, I felt a chill up my spine. It seemed fitting that he'd had such an affinity for the wind. The night he passed, I had felt the turbulence of the hurricane rocking my plane, and now the wind was rocking my body as I stood next to the ocean.

I shifted on the rock and lowered to a crouch, removing the small box with the tiny plastic bag of dust inside. I blinked, the rain tickling my lashes. I thought about the last time I saw him, his body no longer containing his light. I remembered my friend Kristen had warned that when she'd spread her dad's ashes at the ocean the ashes had blown back at her. I didn't want ashes in my face so I carefully opened the bag, which was difficult with the wind. I shifted my position and let go, watching the wind carry the ashes over the top of the incoming waves before the waves enveloped them and swallowed them whole.

I held my hand to my heart. "Goodbye, Nate," I whispered into the wind, tears streaming down my face.

A final gust of wind swirled around me, then stopped. The air became still. The rain stopped, and a beam of light broke through the clouds. I wiped my tears and tried to smile; it all felt surreal. I could feel him sending me a message I could understand. *It's all going to be okay.*

I slowly walked back to my vehicle, and I spent the next hour listening to beautiful soothing meditation music while I watched the waves break against the rocks, the lighthouse towering on the hillside above. I wrote about my experience in the notepad on my phone. I needed a moment to process everything before driving away. Time to regulate my nervous system.

I had said goodbye and told him I would be okay, though I wasn't completely convinced I was ready. I didn't know how I would get there, but I knew that I needed to find a new therapist to start.

Winter had pressed in heavier than before, settling into my chest like a weight I couldn't shake. The layered losses of the season lay thick across my days, a steady, relentless snowfall.

Letting go was not a single act, I realized; it was a season. One that came in waves, in heartbreaks, in quiet surrenders. I had no map for this part of the journey, only a fragile thread of trust that somewhere beyond the grief, beyond the endings, another spring would come. And when it did, I would be ready to reach for it, even with trembling hands.

Chapter 15
Emerging Light

Two years later, in May of 2017, I turned forty-two. I was another year older, but more than that, another season of renewal had arrived: spring, the time of awakening, of seeds pressing through the dark soil reaching for the warmth of the sun. I, too, felt that stirring within me, an urge to grow, to break through the familiar and step into the unknown. Just as the seed must push through resistance to bloom, I realized I needed to challenge myself, to stretch beyond what I knew and embrace the discomfort of growth.

With this desire to expand, I committed to hiking 242 miles, seeking out trails I had never explored before. In the past, I had stayed within the comfort of familiar paths—the ones that felt like home, where I knew every turn, every bridge, every rock that had become a marker of memories. I returned to those places because they felt safe. But pushing myself beyond that space of knowing transformed me.

Fear of the unknown had long been a driving force of my anxiety. My mind would spiral through dozens of worst-case scenarios before I even reached the trailhead. What if I was too slow? Too winded? Too weak? What if I was left behind?

External voices echoed my internal fears: "Be careful out there! Don't go alone! Carry protection." The weight of it all threatened to hold me back. But I was learning through therapy and through my own persistence to reframe my thoughts. To not let anxiety be the one in control.

At the start of each hike, I'd declare, "First hill!" This mantra acknowledged the initial burn, the moment of reckoning. Even on flat trails, the "first hill" wasn't just physical; it was the surge of doubt, the whispers of self-criticism. *What am I doing here? I don't belong. I'm too out of shape. Do I even like hiking?* At times that moment of doubt lasted through an entire hike. Other times I would push past it, only to laugh at myself later—why had I been so worried? By the time I reached the end of the trail, I would rejoice, celebrating my resilience with a smile and a well-earned meal, already anticipating the next adventure.

At the beginning of the year, I had wanted to retreat into my well-trodden paths. There, first hills felt familiar, predictable. I could anticipate every landmark, every resting spot. But something in me was restless. The anticipation of the unknown terrified me, but I had to push forward. I researched obsessively—reading trip reports, studying maps, immersing myself in every detail of a new trail to soothe the anxiety that came with stepping into unfamiliar territory. Preparing became my anchor. I took a navigation class at REI and a mountaineering first aid course with the Mountaineers, and carried my ten essentials no matter the distance. I equipped myself with the tools to quiet the voice of fear, proving to myself that I could handle whatever lay ahead.

Each new trail became a lesson in trust—not just in my preparation, but in myself. I learned to hike alone, to pause when anxiety tightened my chest, to breathe through the uncertainty. That year I hiked seventy-five trails, sixty-eight of them completely new to me. That meant seventy-five first hills, seventy-five moments of doubt, seventy-five opportunities to push through and discover what lay beyond. And each time, I proved to myself that I was capable. That the unknown wasn't something to fear but something to embrace.

I had spent years limiting myself to the same handful of trails, believing they were enough. But I had been wrong. There were mountains I had yet to climb, rivers I had yet to cross, alpine lakes where sunlight danced like scattered diamonds, and snow-covered forests exhaling a soft soothing breath. So much beauty, so much life, waiting just beyond the edge of what I knew. All I had to do was take the first step, and I did. Then I took thousands more, each one carrying me further, until I could feel myself growing in ways I never imagined.

Trail after trail, step after step, I pushed to places that once would have terrified me. Each summit climbed, each mile trekked, was a quiet defiance against the fears that once ruled my world. I prepared, I practiced, I learned. But more importantly, I trusted.

Little by little, the anxious hum inside me began to soften, replaced by a steadier rhythm: a deepening belief that I could carry myself through the unknown.

By the time I reached the end of that year, I realized it hadn't just been the miles that mattered. It was the way I had stretched, the way I had reached, the way I had allowed myself to grow. Somewhere along the ridgelines and riverbeds, I had become something new: not fearless, but braver; not broken, but deeply, beautifully whole.

Chapter 16
Sacred Free Fall

One summer morning, gentle and golden, I awoke to hear birdsong threading through the open window as the summer breeze stirred the curtains. I stretched beneath the soft sheets, wiggled my toes, and let myself soak in the rare, peaceful start to the day.

For a few suspended moments, everything felt light, untouched, full of promise. I had no idea that before the day was done, old ghosts would rise, and I would be called to choose how I would meet them.

Reaching for my phone, I noticed the date: July 28. Instantly my body was transported back in time to another July 28, standing alone in the Seattle hospital waiting room—the sterile walls, the hum of distant voices, the doctor's expressionless face as he told me Nate had cancer. The weight of that moment settled over me, even as the birds continued their song outside.

My body recalled the feelings as if there was no separation of time and space. I felt startled; I hadn't even thought about the date. After Nate passed, I knew that some dates would be harder than others. I'd read about how the cells in the body could hold on to an imprint of past traumatic events; the energy would become trapped and cellular memory would retain things that the brain may not be aware of. Was this one of those moments for me? I had worked for the last several years to change some of those cell memories. When

I knew that hard trigger dates were approaching, I was extra kind to myself. As birthdays, holidays, and anniversaries approached, I'd book massages, invite friends over for joyful theme gatherings, eat super clean, and get more rest. I learned to listen to what my body needed to feel good. Usually the anticipation of a hard date was a lot worse than the actual date. Each year the list of dates would come and go, and it felt a little easier each time because I created new memories in my cells and mind. Grief would come in waves— sometimes they were gentle lapping waves, and other times I'd get blindsided by a whole tsunami while I was looking in the other direction.

On this day, I was pummeled by a tsunami without warning. In the last six years, July 28 had never affected me. It hadn't even been on my radar as a potential hard day.

My body shook, and I lay back down. My mind raced over past and current events, tears streaming down my face. My phone chimed, and I picked it up.

Through blurry eyes, I saw it was my friend Andrea texting. "Hey lovely, how are you today?"

Tears continued to stream down my face as I responded, "It's a really rough morning, and I'm struggling."

Immediately, my phone rang.

"What's up?" I heard the concern in Andrea's sweet, soothing voice.

I told her about my experience and how unexpected it was.

"A group of us are going skydiving today, come join us!" she insisted.

Nausea suddenly crept in on top of all the other feelings I was experiencing. "I'm not sure I can jump out of an airplane. I think I would throw up on myself," I responded.

Her voice softened, seeming to offer compassion for my emotional space. "Okay, well, let me know. We would love to have you join us, but I understand if you don't."

I told her I would let her know and spent the next part of the morning going back and forth in my mind. A mixture of excitement, nervousness, nausea, and anxiety swirled inside me. *Should I do it? Should I not do it?*

I thought about when I was younger and how much I had wanted to go skydiving. I recalled a conversation with my grandpa. "Someday, I am going to go skydiving!" I told him. My grandpa had laughed and asked me why I would jump out of a perfectly good airplane. At some point between then and now, the anxiety had taken over and I hadn't thought about skydiving for years.

I sat and stared at my cell phone screen, determined that I would do it, rationalizing away my fears.

Andrea picked up the phone and I quickly blurted, "I'm going to do it! I figure I will either cause more trauma for the date or else I'll override it with something exciting."

She laughed. "Okay, I'm glad! You can ride with us."

As I left, I grabbed an extra pair of clothes (because I really was expecting to throw up on myself) and locked my front door behind me.

From the back seat of Andrea's car, I hugged my change of clothes against my chest and looked out the window at the large white metal building at the edge of the runway with the word "Skydive" painted in red. I released my grip on the extra clothes, and suddenly felt embarrassed for bringing them. I placed them on the seat, thinking I would come back for them if I needed them. I exited the car, my legs weak as we walked as a group to the closed door.

Inside, I signed the waiver and paid the fee for the jump, checking the box for the video experience. There were six of us and we gathered in the large bay, and I felt the warm air from the open doors. We formed a circle and listened to the orientation of what to do and what to expect as we were each fitted for a harness and gear.

A camera man circled around me. "Hey Angie, how's it going?"

My mind raced, trying to come up with an acceptable answer. "Great!" I lied, a big smile covering the intense emotions I felt deep inside—grief, loss, and nausea.

"Why's it going great?" he asked.

Again, my mind raced. *I'm not great. I'm trying to make it great. Why would I be great?* "Because I'm alive," I blurted out.

Rewrite!

Not because I had been through a traumatic experience but because I had the choice to write a new story for this date. Not to erase the past but to rewrite the present and future. After all, I *was* alive, and I had seen firsthand that none of us are guaranteed anything more than this moment.

I was introduced to my tandem instructor, and he reassured me that everything would be fine and that he would help remind me of all the procedures along the way. I smiled at my friends as we entered the small plane, and I could feel my anxiety elevate. I kept reminding myself that anxiety and excitement have a similar feeling. *Go with the excitement*, I thought.

As the plane took off, I had this overwhelming feeling that I should back out, telling myself that I could decide not to jump and just land with the plane. I looked around nervously, noticing a sign at the front that read NO TURNING BACK NOW.

I took a deep breath as I realized I was holding my breath, and I suddenly felt detached from my body. My free fall videographer asked me some questions to add to my video and I tried my best to appear calm and cool, while inside I imagined this was how a deer felt, standing in the headlights of an oncoming car.

We continued to gain altitude and there was some movement. The door opened, and I could see the ground below us. *This is not a normal thing*, I thought. *You don't just go up in a plane and open the door!* The ground was *really* far away—13,000 feet someone said.

One of my friends moved toward the open door, attached to his tandem instructor. Overwhelmed with anticipation, I felt as if I was floating above myself, my head like a balloon, attached to my body only by a thin string and swaying somewhere above. My mind tried to grasp what was happening. *Maybe this is just a dream.* I could barely feel my feet as I walked slowly toward the wide-open plane door. *This is too much. What am I doing?*

"On the count of three, jump," my instructor said into my ear, seemingly amused.

He tilted my head back and began to count, "One . . . two . . ." and suddenly, without a three, we stepped out of the plane and accelerated to 120 miles per hour, free-falling for sixty seconds.

I had expected to feel my stomach drop, like on a roller coaster, but I experienced only a calm transfer from one space to the next. *I'm doing it—I just jumped out of a plane!* I thought.

"Wooooooo!" I yelled as a sudden blast of wind shot up my nose, my head tightening with that strange, pressurized ache — like the sky itself was hugging my skull too tight. It was that familiar mountain pass sensation, as if my brain had been vacuum-sealed like a bag of chips at high elevation.

I needed to clear my ears. I struggled to pull my hand in toward my face, then plugged my nose and pushed air into my nose until I felt the release of pressure in my ears. What followed was absolute peace and calm. It was a quiet fall, filled with pure bliss, and at about 5,000 feet, the parachute opened with a gentle swoosh as I began to glide.

"Here, grab these . . ." The instructor gently placed his hands over mine as my hands closed around the handles of the parachute.

"Go ahead," he said with a laugh, "you get to drive!"

"Really?" I laughed too, nervous.

"Yep, go ahead like this," he instructed as he pulled on the handles to turn us to the left and then to the right.

His hands let go of mine. I steered us in a circle, pointing out the Olympic Mountains and the glorious Mount Rainier on the horizon, soaking in every moment of the journey down. It was a beautiful blue-sky day with the warmth of the sun shining on my face. Within minutes, we prepared to land in the drop zone, and we gave each other a high five. I felt a bit dazed by the entire experience.

My grandpa's voice rang in my ears. *Why would you jump out of a perfectly good airplane?*

Because, Grandpa. Because why not! Jumping out of a perfectly good airplane that day turned out to be a positive experience.

I hoped that in the years to come, when I saw July 28 on the calendar, the memory of the hospital would still be there, but no longer as a free fall into grief. Instead, I wanted it to be wrapped in the steady embrace of a parachute, the healing experience that softened the descent. I faced the trauma, sat with it, and then chose to redefine it, replacing distress with exhilaration, fear with freedom. My body had held on to the past for so long, but now I had given it something new to hold: the rush of the wind, the weightlessness of possibility, and the reminder that even in free fall, I could find my way back to solid ground.

July 28 had started with a feeling—sharp, unwelcome, and impossible to explain. My body remembered what my mind had tried so hard to bury. Six years collapsed into an instant, the separation of time and space dissolving inside me. The fear, the hurt, the grief, they lived quietly in the hidden corners of my cells, waiting for a crack in the morning's peace to pour through.

I had a choice how I would face the ghosts.

I said yes.

Maybe because healing sometimes demands boldness.

Maybe because life, with all its fragility, deserves a leap of faith. As the ground fell away and the sky opened wide around me, I trusted that the parachute would catch me. Just as I needed to trust that even in the free fall of this season, something unseen would hold me up. I jumped not because I was fearless but because I was alive— and none of us are promised another moment.

Chapter 17

Letting Grow

The leap from the airplane had been a choice. To trust. To let go. To live fully. I didn't know then that another kind of letting go was quietly approaching. One that would stretch my heart in ways even a free fall through the sky could not prepare me for. This time, it was my son Max. My once-tiny boy who had filled my arms and my life with a new kind of love, now standing on the threshold of his own great adventure.

Eighteen years before Max left for college, I had prayed for him before he even existed. That morning, longing for motherhood, I'd sent a silent plea to the universe for a sign. A mysterious knock at my door, a visit from the fire department, and a week later a positive pregnancy test. The first signs of a season about to bloom.

Pregnancy was spring, full of anticipation, growth, and a love so deep it rooted itself into my soul. Motherhood was summer, vibrant and warm, days filled with laughter, bedtime stories, and shared coffee shop moments. Max was my constant companion, my greatest teacher, the sun in my sky.

Then came autumn, the shift, the letting go. As Max prepared for college, I felt the chill of change. I was proud of him, of his clarity and ambition, but the ache settled in. A quiet grief for the empty space he would leave behind. It was the same grief I had met before, the anticipatory kind, the one that builds before the loss even arrives.

We unloaded his packed car into his new apartment, I hugged him tight, and we waved at each other as I drove away. I cried the entire two-hour drive home, already missing him.

Motherhood had been my first great love story, a journey filled with anticipation, joy, and countless everyday miracles. Watching Max step boldly into his future, chasing his passions and creating a life he loved, brought a pride so fierce it almost hurt. Yet tucked inside that pride was a quiet ache—a grief not for him but for the part of me that would now have to learn to live differently.

In every ending, I realized, there is a beginning. Just as I had given Max the tools to fly, I, too, was being called to rise. To embrace this new chapter with open hands and an open heart. Life was shifting again, asking me to loosen my grip, to trust the unfolding, and to step forward into a new kind of beginning.

Chapter 18
Tethered Hope

Seeds first sprout roots and shoots when given the right conditions—moisture, warmth, and time. They push through the soil, fragile but determined, growing leaves and stems until, at last, buds emerge, preparing to unfurl into full bloom.

The seeds within me—seeds of healing, resilience, and self-discovery—needed their own nurturing conditions. I found them in the quiet embrace of nature, tending to my physical and mental well-being, and in allowing myself to soften into the darkness, trusting that spring always came. With rest and intention, I knew I could push through even the heaviest of life's burdens and emerge, once again, into the light.

I felt vibrant and strong, as though my petals were on the verge of opening. I was cultivating a life that supported my well-being, giving myself the care and space needed to thrive. Despite the waves of anticipatory grief surrounding Max and the emotional rewrite I had undertaken by leaping from a perfectly good airplane, I felt whole.

Reframing my thoughts, I chose to see life as happening *for* me, not *to* me. I realized that the anticipation of the jump is often more terrifying than the actual jump, and what comes after the jump has the potential to be greater than I ever imagined. My roots deepened as my community grew. Local connections strengthened, friendships flourished, and I spent more time outside, breathing the expansiveness of the world. My heart felt lighter. I felt my radiance shining brightly. I was on the edge of bloom.

They say when you're just minding your business, not looking for love, that's when it happens. I had tried to date occasionally, thinking I was ready, and I hadn't been. Five years after Nate passed, I met a man named Vic on social media. He had red hair and green eyes that were framed by long, eyelashes.

Vic and I casually exchanged messages from late summer into winter. We intended to meet in person, but we had several missed connections over that first five months. He lived part-time at his home not far from mine, and he spent the rest of his time out of state for work. We never seemed to be in the same place at the same time. When he was home, I was out backpacking in the mountains, or with friends. If I was home, he was busy, sick, or had other plans.

As winter unfolded, it felt unfamiliar. I wasn't experiencing the usual lull that winter often brought. My radiance continued into the dark months, my light shining like a beacon. I still experienced insomnia, but I was embracing the sleeplessness and felt a sense of peace.

That December, I took a spontaneous last-minute trip to Iceland with my friend Melinda. Melinda and I spent a week traveling around Iceland in snow and ice and slept in the back of our rental car. We spent the short four-hour window of winter daylight driving to as many parts of the country as we could.

Melinda and I explored Iceland with a whirlwind of enthusiasm, rushing from place to place. I was wide-eyed and eager to soak it all in. The December sky was a breathtaking mix of contrast and mystery. During the scarce hours of daylight, the sun hovered low on the horizon and cast a soft, golden pink hue over the landscape, often blending with shades of lavender and icy blue.

The nights were long as the sky transformed into a deep blue-black canvas for the tiny glimmers of twinkling stars, so close I could almost touch them. A few nights, the sky was adorned with the shimmering dance of the northern lights. Waves of electric green erupted behind hillsides and reflected on icy waters.

I was captivated by the magic of the night sky in Iceland. I also became captivated as my text conversations with Vic deepened while I lounged in the back of the rental car, waiting for aurora notifications tucked into the warmth of my sleeping bag. Vic and I shared music recommendations, and I would play the songs on the car speakers. We talked about our values, interests, dreams, and goals. Melinda would occasionally tease me for the big grin on my face as she too was busy exchanging texts of her own.

As my time in Iceland came to an end, the conversations with Vic over the last week had confirmed that we both shared values of kindness and honesty. Family was important to us and so were friends, and we both loved our work. We talked about how we would soon dance and climb mountains together.

It felt good to find someone who aligned well, and who wanted to enjoy the same things together. Vic and I agreed that we needed to stop missing these connections and finally meet for tea when I was back in town.

The morning after I returned from Iceland, I drove to a local coffee shop to meet Vic for the first time in person. Vic and I sat across from one another at a small bar-height table. I felt calm and confident as I held my paper cup, steaming from my hot tea. My calm felt new. In my past interactions with men, my anxiety would ramp up and warning lights would go off that I should run. Not this time.

"I am so happy we finally get to meet in person!" I told him as I smiled and carefully sipped my hot tea.

I watched as he looked around the room and noticed how thick his lashes were, framing his eyes. He sat sideways on his seat facing away from me and didn't look at me.

"I am too!" He gazed at the table next to us. "Tell me more about Iceland," he said, smiling down at his paper cup and playing with the plastic lid.

I enthusiastically shared more about Iceland: stories about how Melinda and I got chased down in a field because we'd taken a wrong turn, and how we slept on a frozen pond one night in our car, not realizing it until morning.

I asked questions and he would turn the questions back on me. I tried to make eye contact, but he seemed to look everywhere but at me. He had told me in our texts that he had some social anxiety. I was familiar with anxiety; in the past, I had been uncomfortable in these settings too. I felt grounded and balanced in my growth, and I was proud of myself for the shift I felt in confidence.

Over the next couple weeks, Vic and I spent time together at the local wildlife refuge and enjoyed some short local hikes. He still avoided eye contact, and the connection I felt through our texting and phone interactions seemed to dissolve in person. I left windows of opportunity open as we hung out over the next couple of weeks. I tried gauging his interest, only to feel more confused. Vic was different in person, and I questioned if I had read more into it than there really was.

When he flew out of town for work, his texts became flirty again.

Confused, I texted, "Okay, you might think this is silly, but sometimes when we're texting, I feel like you're being flirty with me, as if you like me."

"Oh, I do!" he replied.

"You do?" I questioned.

"Yes!"

"Like as more than a friend?"

"Yes!" he said.

"I like you more than a friend too!"

"Oh good! I wanted to say something when I was there, but I wasn't sure if you liked me that way, and I didn't want to ruin our friendship if you didn't feel the same way," he wrote back.

I paused. "I was thinking the same thing about you. I think my radar is broken." It had been so long since I had been in a relationship, I wasn't sure how to read the situation.

"I think my radar is broken too, Angie."

We continued to text and video chat over the next month while Vic was away at work, both open to a deeper relationship together.

"I can't wait to see you in person again." I smiled at his face on my phone screen.

"Me too," he said, smiling back.

"I'm thinking about coming to see you." I rubbed my cheekbones. My face hurt from smiling so much.

"Oh, I wish you would!" he responded.

"Okay! I will!" I beamed.

He said several times that it would be great for me to come and visit him. Later that day, I booked a flight and an Airbnb.

When I called to tell him, I said, "Guess what . . ."

"What?" he replied.

"I just booked a plane ticket to come see you! I'll be there in three weeks!"

"Oh wow, really?" he said.

"Yep! Surprise! I figured I would take some time to come explore. If you end up busy, I can find plenty of adventures myself, but I would love to see you!"

"I might have to fly out for a job"—he paused—"but I'll try to be here!"

Did I hear hesitation in his voice or was that my anxiety? I hoped I'd made the right decision. "It's okay, I hope it works out, but I understand if you get called out for work."

I felt brave to risk the unknown, to fly alone, to expand my horizons, and to do it with an open heart. But I was also concerned that he didn't really want me there. *That's silly*, I thought. *He told me he wished I would come see him.* It had to be in my head.

Three weeks went quickly, and when I exited the plane, I found my way to baggage claim. While I waited I looked around, suddenly nervous. Vic popped out from behind a large airport advertisement and yelled, "Surprise!"

I nervously hugged him, and it felt awkward. The last time we were together had left us both confused about how we felt about one another. Our in-person interactions had been distant compared to our texts. This would be our chance to see how the chemistry was between us.

After a brief stop at my Airbnb to drop off my luggage, we drove to a couple of his favorite spots and watched a beautiful sunset. He pulled me close for a selfie, then another. I turned to look at him and noticed he was standing on a rock; I quickly tucked myself into his chest as he took another picture of us together. He was shorter than me, and I wondered if it bothered him. So many men in my past had commented on my height with a tone that made me feel like it was a flaw. Vic didn't seem to mind, a big smile on his face as he extended his arm to take our photo.

The next few days flew by as we explored local parks and ate at some of his favorite restaurants. The two of us navigated trails and laughed. I made him a copycat sandwich from his favorite restaurant in Washington and cooked some tomato soup in my Jetboil on one of our hikes, savoring the flavors as we enjoyed the views.

Still, I couldn't help but notice that our interactions were subdued in person versus at a distance. I felt anxious and confused, and I discounted it as my anxiety of unknowns.

A month after I returned to Washington, he was laid off from his job and returned to his house down the road. I was glad for more time together and was excited to finally do the things we talked about, to introduce him to my family and friends, to hike, to dance, to adventure together. He told me he was excited for those things too.

Vic and I spent much of the next year together, but we weren't doing the things we'd been so excited for. In some ways, he treated me like his girlfriend: He held my hand, took me out to dinner, opened my car door, and wanted to spend most of his free time with me. But our relationship was lacking—there was no intimacy, no overnights, no labels. He insisted he was still processing his last breakup. He was too anxious to meet my family and friends, hikes were limited to short walks, and he admitted that he didn't dance.

The push-pull dynamic over that first year was difficult for me, and I experienced the conditions around me as a harsh winter unlike the gentle uplift I'd had the last winter. I felt the pull downward, as I questioned my worth and if I was asking too much too soon.

I had high hopes that the spring would be better, but Vic still couldn't commit to a label. If I asked for more, he would disappear, only to reappear days or a week later as if nothing happened. I set boundaries; he would break them. When I tried to end the relationship, he would show up with flowers, balloons, stuffed animals, and handwritten cards.

Vic seemed to want me when I became disinterested in continuing a relationship, but he wanted nothing to do with me when I asked for more. It was a harsh dynamic on my heart, and I felt continually pulled between the promises and the reality.

I started to pick apart who I was and internalized all the possible reasons why he would reel me in then discard me, why he would never stay the night, and why I felt like I was often on his last nerve or a burden when I asked for the most basic things. I questioned my worth, my appearance, and my personality. I wondered if I was too much or not enough. He often told me that I wasn't like other girls he'd dated; his type was typically pretty, petite, blonde girls. I felt like a secret kept hidden and I wondered if it was because I wasn't pretty, petite, or blonde.

I loved to eat, and he pointed out that I ate a lot or too quickly. Once, he called me a *"peeeeeeg"* and then defended himself by saying that he didn't call me a pig. He exaggerated the e sound as he said, "No, I called you a *peeeeeeeeg*—that's different."

He insisted that I was overreacting when I told him that was mean.

I tried to make sense of it all. He told me that I was just too sensitive.

Maybe I was too sensitive.

Maybe I misunderstood him.

As time went on, I realized that our heartfelt conversations about our shared interests and values in the beginning had been all talk.

"I really was being honest with you," he said. "Those *were* things I wanted to do and who I *want* to be."

"So, you were telling me a story of who you wanted to be, not who you really are?" I was upset. "We talked about this, and I said in the beginning that it was very important to me that you were honest about who you are. I've always been honest with you. I told you exactly who I am, what I've been through; I held nothing back, even when I was scared or thought you would reject me, because I would never want someone to love me for who I'm not."

"I *will* be those things. I'm just not there *yet*," Vic insisted.

"The problem is you weren't honest about who you are, and this push-pull between us just doesn't work for me. You're either not ready for a relationship or just not with me. I can't continue like this."

"Don't go. I just need a little more time, Angie. I'm close. You're the one I want to be with. I'm just not there yet to say the words," he said. "And I really do want to do all those things with you, and I want to be all those things for you. I'm trying."

I had planted seeds of hope, believing they would bloom into something lasting. I had sprouted new roots, trusting that love, real love, would take hold if I gave it enough time, enough patience, enough of myself. In the beginning, I shined so brightly. My own light reflected back at me in every adventure, every promise of "almost." But slowly, almost gradually, that light began to flicker under the weight of trying to be enough for someone who had not yet become who he promised to be.

Every time I tried to pull away, he reached for me, offering just enough to tether my heart a little longer. I held on, caught between defeat and hope. Convincing myself that maybe, if I waited just a little longer, he would finally become the person I needed him to be. But deep down, I began to understand. Love should not lie on the cusp. Love should not leave you always reaching. And while the roots I had planted were strong, I was beginning to see that not everything that grows is meant to stay.

Chapter 19
Drifting Tides

Memorial Day weekend arrived wrapped in the scent of summer and possibility. I had longed for this, a few quiet days beside the ocean as I had done the last few years. The steady pull of the tides. The endless stretch of sand dissolving into the sky. I imagined falling asleep under a canopy of stars, the lullaby of the waves crashing away the weight I carried. I wanted it to be a trip shared, a moment of peace together.

"Let's backpack together to the beach." I zealously enticed Vic with further description. "We can look at tide pools at low tide, relax during high tide, and best of all, enjoy each other's company," I said, grinning at him. "Winter has been rough for me, and I soooooooooo need this! Plus, I've got extra gear that you can use."

I needed the magic of the beach and hoped that it would help us to feel closer. I worried that he would say no; the familiar knot had already formed in my stomach before I even brought it up.

"Yeah, sure," he said, smiling back.

I bounced to my feet and clapped my hands with excitement. "Yay!"

I quickly hurried to the garage door and pulled out the extra overnight pack from the shelf for him to try on. As I upgraded my gear over the years, I'd saved the old gear in hopes that someday I would have someone to adventure with me.

He looked at me, confused. "I thought we were going to camp in your Jeep."

"Oh, no! This is backpacking! It's a short hike down to the beach, and we can camp *on* the beach! Ooooooh it's so lovely to sleep with the sound of the waves so close!" I swooned.

I saw the light bulb go on for him. "Oh, okay."

That afternoon, I went to the grocery store. I strategically navigated the aisles to select foods that I knew he would love. Vic was picky about what he ate, and I had become quite skilled at choosing foods he would enjoy for our adventures. I carefully packed both overnight packs and placed most of the weight in my pack: our gear, extra water, bacon and eggs, pizza, cupcakes. I packed his with an extra sleeping bag, leaving room for his essential body pillow and personal items. I wanted him to enjoy his first backpacking trip, and he wasn't used to so much weight on his back like I was.

The evening before the trip I texted him, "Will it work to pick you up at 6 a.m. tomorrow so we can make it to the trailhead around 10? I'm excited to get my favorite spot."

"Where are we going again? And for how long?" he asked.

I paused. I had been very clear about the details, but sometimes Vic forgot things. I prayed that he wasn't going to back out.

I sent him the details again and took a deep breath and held it as I sent a follow-up message: "I really need this."

I hoped that adding what it meant to me would keep him on board with going. *Please don't back out,* I whispered as I watched my phone, willing the message to land on his heart and hoping he would still go. I felt my anxiety creeping in, and my heart raced.

I heard the *vwooop* sound as his text arrived. "That's too far to drive and it's boring out that way, there's nothing to see. Let's drive east instead."

"This is important to me," I replied. "I've been looking forward to this since last year, and you said you would go with me." I bit my lip and closed my eyes after I hit send. He didn't do well with pressure.

My phone lit up with his reply: "I changed my mind. I'm just going to stay home."

I saw it coming, yet I still felt crushed. This wasn't the first time he'd changed his mind. As much as I tried not to pressure him, ultimately it was always too much for him.

I didn't want to pressure Vic, even now. I didn't want him to go if he didn't want to, but I wanted him to *want* to go.

When his yes turned into a no, I realized something more painful than disappointment: I could no longer count on him. If I wanted peace, if I wanted freedom, I would have to find it on my own.

I felt my excitement replaced with fear. Fear of going alone. Panic. Overwhelm. I had never gone backpacking alone. If I had known earlier, I could have invited other friends to go. I knew that inviting others would have been an instant no from him. Now, I was faced with a decision. To stay or to go?

"K," I texted quickly. "Have a good weekend."

My text was laced with hurt as I felt the door shut to my heart.

The next morning, I woke up, hopeful he had changed his mind. I hoped for a text saying, "Hey Angie, I know this is important to you. I want to go." But my phone was silent, no further conversation.

The early dark of morning outside, I hoisted my heavy pack into the Jeep and drove the four hours to the coast.

The long drive solo taunted my anxiety. It was hard for me to drive long distances alone, and my mind reeled with anxiety, with anger, with scorn. I silenced notifications from Vic and thought about how I deserved better than this. I wasn't asking him to do everything with me, but I was always quick to agree to what he wanted to do, and if he said that something was important to him, I would bend over backward to be there for him.

This was the first time I had stuck to my plan, with or without him. It was clear to me that my needs didn't matter to him.

I parked my Jeep in the gravel lot and pulled my pack onto my back. I felt the extra weight on my back paired with the burden of my heavy heart. I took a deep breath and lifted my chin up. *I got this—his loss. I deserve better,* I thought. *Whatever.*

My heart ached.

I spent three days and two nights on a beautiful rocky beach, the weather surprisingly sunny and hot for the Washington coast. I painted images of the rocky coastline on thick paper with watercolors, and my mind raced with thoughts of the past year: his actions, his behaviors; my actions, my behaviors. I became increasingly angry—angry with Vic for consistently letting me down, and angry with myself for consistently staying. I was smart, I recognized the things he said and did, and I deserved someone who was able to show up for me. I was ashamed I'd held out hope that he could be the person he said he was. He had given me enough moments to breadcrumb me into thinking that he cared. I needed consistency; I deserved it, and I was worthy of it.

I resisted the urge to check my notifications that I had silenced. He didn't deserve to be part of this.

I stared into the waves as they crashed on the shore, the salty breeze stinging my face. I watched people walk the beach from my cozy nook within a pile of driftwood. I ate more. *He would have loved this bacon,* I thought as I ate the entire contents of the package myself. I wandered tide pools at low tide, music playing in my headphones, but nothing seemed to drown out the loop of thoughts. I built a driftwood fire and poked the coals as it snapped and popped. I made cupcakes and watched the sun set over the ocean; the warm glow of the fire embers flushed my cheeks.

The next afternoon, I changed into my bikini and lay down in the sand behind a driftwood log, hidden from view. The sand warmed me from below and I shifted to move the sand around my body, creating the perfect cradle for my curves. I hated that I was there alone. *I deserve a healthy relationship where the person I'm with claims me as their girlfriend and shows up when it's important—maybe even when it's not important.*

I felt a little bit brave for going anyway.

I dozed off to sleep and felt something tap against my skin. I swiped my hand across my bare stomach, my eyes still shut. I felt the tap again. I opened my eyes this time and saw a silhouette of a person tossing pebbles at me, the image illuminated by the sun. Startled, I sat up quickly and realized it was my friend Mike.

"Mike!" I exclaimed. "What in the world . . ."

Mike sat down. "You know, that was a really long walk after having knee surgery."

"Holy cow, you're here!" I stood and gave him a big hug.

The night before, I had told him I was backpacking alone because Vic had backed out at the last minute. Mike had said that he was worried about me, and to let him know when I arrived safely, which I had.

"Why are you here? I told you I was okay." I waved my hand around to show him my camp, settling on the driftwood log beside him.

"I just wanted you to know what it felt like to have someone drive four hours one way and hike a mile and a half after having knee replacement surgery for you." He gave me a side hug. "Even if it's just for an hour."

I smiled and took a deep breath. "Thank you, I feel cared for."

For the next hour, we sat and watched the ocean, my knees hugged to my chest, old friends talking about life, love, and heartache.

"You know you deserve better, right?" he said as he stood to leave.

"I know, right?" I responded with a hint of sarcasm.

He gave me a hug. I could feel my back crack, his arms squeezed me so tight. "You have so much value, Angie—never forget that."

"Thanks, Mike. So do you." I hugged him back and watched him make his way down the beach before the high tide, a water bottle tucked into his back pocket.

I pulled on an extra layer of clothes and grabbed my sleeping bag. I sat in the sand, the driftwood log at my back, and watched the sun set over the ocean, the bright orange flooding the piles of driftwood along the shore and sending a soft glow into the trees. The scattered clouds along the horizon caught the colors and shot fiery beams into the sky, erupting with the dazzling light show that I treasured every time I sat on that beach.

As the final light faded, I climbed into my tiny tent and pulled my sleeping bag up under my chin. I listened to the waves breaking, the sound soothing me. I thought about Mike and how special it felt that he had driven four hours to spend one hour with me. I was thankful that he had been there for me when I needed him.

My soul needed the ocean, the salty air, the respite. I felt proud of myself; I was brave to go alone, and I knew I needed to celebrate this moment for how far I had come. My eyes grew heavy as I was lulled to sleep.

When I pulled into my driveway, a large bouquet of flowers was sitting in front of the garage, balloons attached and swaying in the breeze. Neon green poster board signs were taped to the house with painted words saying how amazing I was. I swooped the bundle into my arms as I entered the garage. I noticed a card attached and opened it as I sat the bright arrangement on the counter. The card was filled with lovely heartfelt words of adoration and gratitude for being such a beautiful, wonderful person. Signed, Vic.

I looked at my phone, clicked on his name, and saw that the silenced notifications had contained dozens of messages from him. Suddenly, I heard the doorknob jiggle, then a key in the door.

Vic walked in after using the spare key I kept under the flowerpot. "Hey, I'm glad you're back—I missed you! How was your trip?"

I was startled by how oblivious he was to my emotional state, but this wasn't new. "I went alone," I responded.

"That's cool!" He smiled as he walked past me into the kitchen.

"Is it? It's the first time I've ever gone backpacking alone!" I felt angry.

"You're welcome! I helped you grow!" he said, still smiling, as he opened the pantry to rummage its contents.

"Yes, you changed my life," I started. "You confirmed that I cannot count on you, and I can only count on myself."

"Ouch." He paused to look at me with a hurt expression on his face as he closed the pantry door.

"It's true, I told you I needed this, and you said it was too boring of a drive. I wanted to spend time with you. Is time driving with me too boring? Is time together not worth the drive? I love you and have been looking forward to this time together, and I had to go alone."

"Oh my fucking God, Angie, what the fuck is wrong with you? I'm sorry but I didn't want to go, and now you're making a big fucking deal about it. What the actual fuck?"

I felt the hot lava spill into my brain chamber and the tingle in my fingertips; my brain was shutting down. My heartbeat quickened, and I could feel the heavy weight on my chest. *How do I respond? What do I say? Was I wrong to expect him to go? Was I overreacting? I can't think. Why am I even angry?* My eyes and chest burned and I closed my eyes, hoping I would disappear. My eyes fluttered open, tears started to fall, and I quickly put my hands over my face. *Breathe*, I thought. *Just breathe.*

I heard footsteps, then "I'm leaving."

The white wooden fish that hung from the back of my door clinked loudly as the door slammed shut. I locked the dead bolt on the front door after retrieving the hidden spare key.

The trip I had envisioned us taking together became my first solo backpacking journey—a journey not just across the sand but into a new kind of self-reliance. I had pitched my tent, tucked into the edge of trees and open sky. I listened to the waves alone and reminded myself that bravery isn't always grand gestures. Sometimes it's simply choosing to stay when you're scared, trusting your own steps when no one else is walking beside you.

My friend's unexpected arrival, just to stand with me for a single hour, showed me a glimpse of the kind of love I deserved. Effort without obligation. Presence without excuses.

But when I returned, Vic's grand gestures missed the heart of what I needed most. His surprise at my hurt, his inability to understand why reliability mattered, left a hollow space between us.

I climbed the stairs heavy with defeat, my body aching not from the miles I had hiked but from the miles growing between us. And when I opened my bedroom door, the air hit me—thick with the scent of his cologne, a smell that burned rather than comforted. He knew I was allergic to scents, especially cologne. It was a final, suffocating reminder: Love cannot be built where respect is missing.

Chapter 20
Boundless Resolve

As spring made way for summer, the days stretched longer, golden and forgiving. I felt the sun kiss my skin, the warmth sinking deep into places that had long been cold. Somewhere between the lengthening evenings and the blooms returning to earth, I made a quiet, fierce decision: I would live my life fully—with or without someone to share it.

My joy. My freedom. My life. They would no longer be conditional; they would now belong to me.

Vic made his usual promises to put more effort into our relationship and wooed me with flowers and cards, enticing me with extensive talks about the meaning of life, the universe, and beyond.

I planned adventures filled with hikes, long weekends overlanding in the back of my Jeep, and any other adventure I felt called to. I left the invitations open to friends and Vic. I always preferred company over going alone, but my heart yearned for adventures and new places.

Occasionally, Vic or friends would join me, but mostly I spent nights out alone.

I converted the back of my silver Jeep Wrangler into a sleep space with a six-inch, full-size mattress and built a platform across the back with a shelf to store items that I would need while camping:

dedicated cooking equipment, shelf-stable snacks, coffee cups, books, and cozy blankets and pillows. The inside had fairy lights strung back and forth. It provided a safe space that I could retreat to on a forest road, trailhead, campground, or public land, lock the doors, and feel somewhat safe.

I loved any opportunity to park in a place where I could wake up, pop the top open on the Jeep, and watch a glorious sunrise before quickly hopping on a trail at first light.

When I stayed overnight somewhere with reception, my phone would light up with sweet text conversations from Vic, much like those from our early moments.

"I miss you, come home," he would text. "I wish I was there with you."

I sat in front of the most beautiful views and still wished I could share it, but I also feared not living my life. I thought about how I wanted to spend whatever time I had left in life. Would I get to the end and be happy with the choices I had made?

I would never regret love, and I would never regret satiating the hunger I had for living the width of my life.

I gained confidence with each new adventure and felt physically capable to climb mountains and explore the world around me alone, but I always felt the steady hum of anxiety within. At times I experienced extreme spikes that would leave me breathless, my brain flooded with possible dangers and drained of energy.

As I pushed on, the anxiety would calm, my breath would return to normal, and I felt more confident in my ability to tackle the dangers or challenges should they manifest themselves.

I let go of the tight grip of yearning to be in a relationship, to experience intimate connection, and instead I tried to find other ways to spend time with Vic with less strenuous activities that he had an interest in. We took short drives, wandered around the hardware store, sat on his porch in conversation about the meaning of life and the vast universe, and attended more and more live music shows together.

I still longed to have an intimate relationship. I craved being seen, heard, considered. I yearned for companionship—hiking, camping, backpacking, simple moments by a campfire or stargazing. I longed to create new memories on holidays, with family, with friends. These things seemed basic to me, but so far from reach.

I tried to rationalize why I kept trying. I knew I had fallen in love with an idea of who Vic said he was. There were glimpses, moments, and promises that made me believe that the image he had painted with words was real. Somewhere. Just on the verge, asking me to hold on just a little bit longer.

I questioned my needs. He had told me my expectations were unrealistic. People I knew said that no one could keep up with me.

Maybe he was right; maybe my friends were right. Maybe this was close enough. Maybe I couldn't expect another person to see me, hear me, spend time with me.

I needed someone to be there for me, to be in a real relationship with at least an acknowledgment that we were in a relationship. I yearned to be held physically and emotionally. I needed to feel loved and know that I could count on the person I loved to show up.

My new therapist, Brandie, suggested I be clear with him on what I needed and set a time limit.

Later that day, I wrote down the conversation I wanted to have and rehearsed it. I had recently recognized that it was hard for me to vocalize my needs. As much as I tried to maintain peace, there had been a lot of conflict in my past, and as a result a raised voice sent my body into survival mode, my brain became emotionally flooded, and I suddenly was unable to think clearly. Trying to communicate in that state was impossible, which led to me just saying, "I don't know," over and over. The person on the other end of the communication would usually get madder at me, their voice elevating more, and sometimes it would become abusive. I really didn't know how to respond; the brain flooding completely shut off my ability to communicate. I would feel so dumb, and it always made people angry. My entire body would become exhausted for hours or days after. I wished that that I didn't get so overwhelmed, and that I could be clear without fear.

Later that day, I was able to get up the courage to gently and clearly tell Vic what I needed and gave him my timeline – the first day of spring.

"That's a lot to process," he said with a dazed look on his face. "I've got to get going, but I'll talk to you later."

"Okay," I said quietly. This was how most of our conversations went. When I wasn't flooded, I said too much, and he ran away. I was always too much. I had to be clear; the boundary had been communicated.

Promises floated easily from Vic's lips, but often they evaporated before they ever took root. Nights that should have been shared slipped by in the back of my Jeep, alone but alive, choosing adventure rather than sitting idle in unfulfilled waiting.

I refused to regret loving him. Love, after all, was never the mistake. But I was tired of carrying the weight of unreturned affection, tired of questioning if wanting partnership, consistency, and care made me "unrealistic."

It didn't.

It made me honest. It made me human.

I drew the line. A timeline. A boundary shaped by self-respect.

As the date approached, confusion gnawed at me. The breadcrumbs he offered were just enough to keep the questions alive. Was he almost ready? Was I asking for too much? Was I enough?

But somewhere deep inside, beneath the flickers of doubt, a new truth began to stir. I realized that love built on "almost" could never fully hold me. The life I was building, sun-drenched, hard-earned, and fiercely mine, deserved more than waiting on promises that might never be kept.

Chapter 21
Unfiltered Truth

The calendar pages turned slowly, each day marked not just in ink but in the quiet, measured beat of my heart. Outside, the first crocuses began lifting the soil, small bursts of purple and yellow daring to rise through winter's final chill. They were nature's gentle nudge toward something new, something alive. And yet, inside me, a different struggle was unfolding. One I hadn't yet seen coming.

A week before the first day of spring, I took the day off from work to tackle some tasks on my growing to-do list. I had turned off my alarm the night before with hopes to catch up on some sleep, but I still woke up at my routine 4 a.m. time. I responded to a couple of texts with my usual 4 a.m. crew, then snuggled closer to my pillow. I pulled the blankets up as I drifted back to sleep with Ruby nestled into my side. An hour later, my eyes opened, and I felt more refreshed than I had in weeks. I grabbed my cell phone off my bed and headed downstairs to make a cup of coffee.

I responded to a text from my mom, "Sorry, I fell back asleep since I have the day off."

She texted back, "Figured you had!"

I placed my coffee mug under the Keurig, put a coffee pod in, and the lid made the familiar snapping sound as it closed. I hit the brew button; my bare feet shifted on the cool wood floor and the edge of my black chemise brushed against my thighs.

I watched as the hot, dark liquid gurgled into my cup. Suddenly, I felt a strong hunger pang. I grabbed my stomach and thought about the yogurt I'd had for a snack before bed, then looked at the clock on the stove. It was still early for breakfast for me; usually I wouldn't eat for another couple hours.

A sharp cramp in my stomach was followed by a wave of nausea. As the coffee sputtered, I walked toward the downstairs bathroom. Suddenly dizzy, I felt my face begin to sweat. My lips tingled and my heart raced—I knew this feeling.

Just a few years before, wearing a fancy ball gown at a masquerade ball, I'd felt the same woozy feeling, the abrupt hunger and face sweating, just before my friend said she saw me fall like a tree on the marble floor of the state capitol building. This time, I was alone in my own house, and I feared that I might be going down.

I'm all alone—no one would even know! I began to panic. *What should I do?* I decided to unlock the front door and grab my phone.

In my last flash of consciousness, I remember moving toward the front door that was located just outside the bathroom. Suddenly, I heard a loud noise, a crash in the distance. My thoughts felt surreal and dreamlike as I wondered about the sound.

When my eyes opened, I could hear Ruby's nails on the hardwood floor as she scampered around my head. I was on the floor. *What is Ruby doing?* I wondered. I lay still for a moment, assessing my body, not knowing how long I had been there. I sat up slowly. I looked at the front door, just a foot from where I lay. I was confused. *Oh, the door. Did I unlock it?* I focused my eyes on the knob. It was still locked, and the dead bolt was in place.

I slowly lifted myself off the floor, unlocked the door, and carefully walked to the kitchen for my phone and dialed my mom.

"Hello?" she answered. I could tell she was confused that I called instead of sending the usual text.

"Mom, I just passed out. I think I just need to eat something, and I'm sure I'm fine. Will you come over and sit with me for a minute?"

"Of course," she replied, "I'll be right over."

I felt relieved that she lived just two miles from me. The last time this happened I went to visit my naturopath and had blood work done. She told me I was fine and I likely had a random low blood sugar moment. She had advised me if I felt faint that I could just eat a LifeSaver or something to get some quick sugar in me, so while I waited on my mom I had a small mandarin orange and poured some granola and almond milk into a bowl.

Mom let herself in and sat on the end of the couch. "Are you okay?"

"Yeah, I must have just needed some food." I shrugged as I took the last bite of granola and slowly stood to put my bowl in the sink. "I'm sure I'm fine. You can go, and I'll let you know if I feel bad again."

"Are you sure?" she asked as she stood and followed me to the kitchen.

"Oh yeah, thanks for coming over, though. I'm sorry you had to come by. I must have had my blood sugar drop, and I'm already feeling better."

"No problem," she said, walking to the front door. "Just let me know if you need anything else."

"I'm just planning on relaxing now, and I'll make sure I get plenty of food and water today. Maybe my to-do list will have to wait," I said, holding the door open as she stood on the porch.

I smiled and waved at her as I shut the door and decided to keep the door unlocked for now. Inside, I lifted my hand to my head to rub the tender spot and I winced.

The next day, I woke up when my alarm began to chime at 4:00 a.m. I slowly walked downstairs to the kitchen, and as my first cup of coffee brewed I made myself some bacon, eggs, and toast. I wasn't going to chance a repeat of the day before. It was a work from home day, so after breakfast, I walked to my home office, my second cup of steaming coffee in hand, and logged into my work laptop.

As I opened each email and read the messages, my energy depleted quickly. I began feeling a stir in my stomach and throat. A queasy, slightly nauseous feeling washed over me, and I got up to replace my cup of coffee with a glass of water. The queasiness continued, even after a glass of water, and I decided to email my boss and tell him that I needed to take the afternoon off. I thought about a nap, maybe some extra rest for the day. I already had Friday off and had only planned to help Vic with some of his work stuff over the weekend.

On Monday morning, I felt better and I drove to the office. As I scrolled through emails and project files on my computer, I began to get sharp piercing pain in my eyes and head. The nausea took over and I walked to the bathroom, afraid I would throw up. *I really hope I'm not coming down with something,* I thought. *I should go home.* The nausea increased on my drive; I felt panic wash over me and wondered if I would make it home, unable to focus on the road or traffic. I was glad that I would be working from home Tuesday and could work from the comfort of my couch.

As the week went on, the nausea increased, and my friends urged me to go to the hospital.

"You could have a brain bleed from passing out, Angie," one friend warned me.

"Oh, my goodness, I don't have a brain bleed," I said. "If I feel worse, I will go to the doctor, okay? Really, I'm fine!"

On Wednesday evening, a week after I had passed out, I stood in Vic's dining room and listed to a conversation between him, his dad, and his cousin. I laughed at something they said, and words came out of my mouth slurred and jumbled. All eyes turned to me, and I nervously laughed and waved it off as if it was nothing.

"I'm just tired," I said, walking to the door.

I knew something was not right in that moment, and I drove home.

Ironically, I was writing a textbook on traumatic brain injury for work, and the signs and symptoms I had experienced for the last week pointed to traumatic brain injury. My brain was so confused, I didn't see the warning signs, even though I was researching and writing about them.

I noticed that my severe headaches and nausea were tied to light and sound—my computer monitor, cell phone, the lighting aisle at the hardware store, the sun, music. Each morning I woke up feeling good, but within an hour I felt like I had been on an all-night bender consuming large amounts of alcohol. I felt drunk; I felt hungover. I experienced nausea, vertigo, and headaches, needing people to whisper because everything felt too loud and anxiety provoking. The action of thinking seemed nearly impossible as I could feel my brain trying to work, which made me even more nauseous and anxious. My job writing textbooks was incredibly mentally demanding between reading journal articles, talking to subject matter experts, and sitting in front of a screen for nine hours a day sorting through data and translating it into digestible, easy-to-read pieces for the future learner—my brain was overwhelmed by the effort it took to work.

Back at my house, I realized I should probably go to the doctor.

"Will you take me to urgent care?" I asked Vic.

"You're fine, you just need to rest," he replied.

"No," I said, "I think I had better just go to make sure."

Vic reluctantly drove me to urgent care and sat in the chair next to me in the examination room. His head pressed against the wall, he sighed loudly. I knew that he didn't care for doctors' offices, and I hoped that it would be quick and I'd be sent home.

"Sorry," I apologized to Vic, waiting for the doctor, "I'm sure this will be quick. I just need to be sure."

"Okay." He slouched down further in his seat and looked at the ceiling, his legs extended in front of him.

He perked up as the doctor entered the room, and I told the story of the morning I passed out. I detailed the week that followed, including the slurring, and explained that this wasn't the first time I'd passed out but it was the first time I'd had these symptoms—that I could recall.

"You need to go to the emergency room right away," the doctor advised.

I looked at Vic, a lump caught in my throat.

"You're fine!" he said as he stood and walked out the front door. I grabbed my purse and rushed after him.

Was he annoyed at me? As we walked out of the urgent care clinic, I felt scared.

"I guess I need to go to the hospital," I said as I sat in the passenger seat of his car.

"You're fine," he repeated, "you don't need to go to the hospital."

As much as I had been trying to act like I was fine, I knew that I wasn't. The symptoms were all too clear now, and with the doctor's confirmation, I knew I had to go.

"I don't want you to have to take me to the hospital, but I really think I need to go," I said, as he navigated his car out of the urgent care parking lot. "If you drop me off at my mom's, I will have her take me."

I searched his face, looking for some kind of compassion. Tomorrow was the first day of spring. I searched for any kind of indication that he cared about me. If I couldn't count on him to support me in these times, then when? Was I really asking too much?

"Okay, if you're sure, I'll take you to your mom's," he said in a familiar tone that said, *Okay, if you're sure I won't hear about this later as another thing I messed up.*

Of course, I'm sure, I thought, a*nd you won't have to hear about this later because there won't be a later.* I wasn't going to beg the person I loved to take me to the emergency room when I had a possible brain injury—or any other injury for that matter. He should have been so concerned for my well-being that the only question was how fast he could get me there.

"I'm sure," I said, nodding, as I texted my mom that I was on my way to her house to get a ride to the hospital.

Vic dropped me off at my mom's house and my mom drove me to the hospital. We entered the large glass doorway into the emergency room and found two seats against a wall. The sound of the "Baby Shark" song blared on the television in the waiting area, slightly muffling the sound of a man moaning in a wheelchair with his head down. I observed the others in the room. A woman in the corner quietly cried as she held her stomach, the man next to her with his arms wrapped protectively around her. A young girl and an older woman sat against a wall of windows, and I watched the young girl hunch over and throw up on the shiny floor; the smell of vomit caused my stomach to contract. I pulled my shirt up over my nose and closed my eyes, afraid I would throw up too. The light, the smells, the sounds—I felt nauseous.

My phone rang; it was Frank, Vic's dad. "Angie, Vic told me that you had to go to the hospital." His voice was thick with worry. "Do you need anything? Are you okay?"

"I'm in the waiting room of the emergency room," I replied. "I'll let you know what I find out."

"You'd better be okay! You *need* to be okay!" he insisted.

I hung up the phone and closed my eyes. My head leaned gently against the wall, and I thought about the amount of time I spent at the house that Vic and his dad shared. Frank was always kind to me.

My phone rang again. This time Vic's name appeared on my screen.

"Dad said I should have taken you to the hospital. I'm so sorry. I can come now and relieve your mom," he said.

"No," I replied. My walls were up. "I'll be fine, Mom is already here. I'll let you know if she needs to go somewhere."

"Do you want me to bring you anything? Some food?" he offered. "I'm sorry I didn't take you. I'm a little slow sometimes."

"No, it's okay. I'll let you know what I find out here."

I hung up quickly. I felt hurt. My brain hurt from my fall, but my heart hurt because it took his dad pushing him to make him offer to come see me. My person would have brought me here.

"Angela?" I heard someone call my birth name. It was my turn.

My mom and I stood and walked to a small intake room where they took my vitals before we were sent to another room where I was hooked to an electrocardiogram (EKG) because they thought there might be something wrong with my heart.

"Hey!" I giggled as the wires were attached to my chest. "I'm a Power Ranger, you going to give me some superpowers?"

The nurse laughed.

I'm pretty funny, I thought. In fact, despite everything going on I felt quite witty.

I waited for hours after my EKG to see a doctor. Eventually, I was taken to a bed in a hallway with a chair for my mom to sit. The hospital was over capacity as I was told it often was, and there were no rooms. I was thankful to just be seen finally. There were other people in the hall on beds too with a range of conditions—some moaning and in obvious pain, others seemingly disoriented, while still others slept.

My pain tolerance is high so I was worried that with the level of pain I experienced it could be very bad. I repeated my story over and over to each person who stopped by—the doctor, the nurse. I had realized that the sounds that morning I had wondered about were first the side of my head hitting the wall, then the back of my head landing on the hardwood floor.

I explained that this was the second time I had passed out, and that the first time witnesses said my body didn't bend or crumple but had gone straight down with force, like a tree. Maybe it was the same this time, only my fall was blocked first by the wall near the bathroom before my five-foot-ten frame crashed immediately into the hardwood floor.

I thought about my previous fall in the capitol building on the marble floor and wondered if I was now experiencing a second traumatic brain injury (TBI). In my research, I'd learned that multiple brain injuries could mean increased risk, leading to longer recovery time and ongoing problems that I hoped wouldn't be the case for me.

The emergency room doctor said they would skip the brain scan and not expose me to unnecessary radiation and that it seemed like my symptoms were improving rather than getting worse. "You've got a concussion," she told me.

I figured as much. A concussion is a mild TBI, and they are caused by a bump, blow, or jolt to the head. In my case, my head smashing into the wall and floor had caused large bruises on the side and back of my brain. I knew that the word "mild" just meant that the injury was not life-threatening, and that the effects could still be very serious.

I should have gone to the hospital sooner; I should have known better. It was concerning that even being in the middle of writing a textbook on TBI, and knowing how serious it can be, my brain was too injured to understand the extent of my injury.

I could have had bleeding in my brain, in which case, things could have been much worse. Sometimes symptoms don't appear for hours or days after the injury. Maybe that was what happened to me, but how could I know since I live alone? My symptoms had progressively worsened, with the final cue for me being the slurred speech in the dining room at Vic's house.

The ER doctor prescribed a limited work schedule and referred me to a specialist. I knew the symptoms and therapies from writing the textbook, and I had already been trying to rest as much as I could.

I kept telling myself that rest time was healing time. The more I could rest and sleep, the faster I would heal. I focused my efforts on developing my superpowers. I listened to podcasts on the amazing healing ability of the brain and tried to remain positive.

There was quite a bit of fear and anxiety underlying my diagnosis. What if I couldn't remember things after this? What if I couldn't do my job? What if I wasn't smart anymore? What if I lost my ability to write and paint and read and ... and ... and ... To combat this fear, I told myself repeatedly, "I am healthy, I am happy, I am healed. Sleep is good. Sleep heals." And if I was going to end up with superpowers after it was all said and done, I hadn't discovered them yet.

The day after I went to the hospital, I had my regular therapy appointment and I decided to drive, against my better judgment. Driving put a strain on my brain, and I was so overwhelmed that I had to pull over several times to close my eyes and calm my brain so the nausea wouldn't take over.

I sat on Brandie's couch and took a deep breath as she looked at me. I knew she anticipated a report on my decision about Vic. It was the first day of spring and it was time to get off the fence.

"Well," I started, "it's been an unexpected couple of weeks."

"Oh? What's been going on?" She looked concerned. I felt like she was one of the few people who could really read me and my body language.

I told her about the concussion and that I didn't feel like I could make any decisions about my life right now. My brain hurt too much to think, let alone have the ability to have the conversation and comprehend any of it.

"At least I didn't lose my sense of humor!" I told her.

She laughed. "What do you mean?"

I told her the story of being hooked up to the EKG and that I was cracking jokes about being a Power Ranger and how hilarious I was.

"Your filter is currently off because of your brain injury," she responded.

"Oh," I said, the amusement leaving my voice.

"This is unfiltered Angie," she explained.

I looked at her and squinted, trying to process what she was saying. "So, you're saying that this is stuff that I would say or do if I didn't care what people thought."

"Exactly! This would be a great time for you to create a vision board. What does unfiltered Angie want?" She encouraged, "You will spend less time overanalyzing it all, and it would become your unfiltered desires for what you want your life to look like."

Interesting. As I left her office, I wondered what unfiltered Angie would come up with.

The concussion forced me to stop, to listen to the broken rhythms inside my own body. It revealed what I hadn't wanted to fully admit—that care, real care, is not a promise spoken but a presence given. Vic's absence in my time of need said more than any words could. In my most vulnerable moments, the choice had been made for me.

As I rested and my mind slowly cleared, I sat down with a blank canvas and an open heart. I created a vision board that wasn't filtered by fear or softened by the hope that someone might change but instead shaped by the truest parts of me. Empathy. Compassion. Being loved through action, not apology. I no longer needed to wonder what I deserved; I could see it laid out plainly before me. My healing had begun, not just from a concussion but from years of trying to bloom where love had not been truly tended.

Chapter 22
Shifting Tides

Two months after my concussion, I still felt like I was moving through water. Disoriented. Heavy. Endlessly tired. Driving was out of the question. Some days I slept twenty hours, my body begging for a healing that my mind could barely keep pace with. Light stabbed at my skull, sounds scrambled my thoughts, and even music, the anchor that had once tethered me to myself, became unbearable noise.

In the quiet moments, when the nausea ebbed and the grief pressed softer against my chest, I thought about the ocean. I pictured the steady rhythm of the waves, the pull of the tide against the sand. The endless sky stretching out above me. I wished for someone who would carry the heavy pack for me, build me a fire, and simply let me heal with the sea as my witness. My concussion doctor gave me quiet permission: Hike if your body allows it.

With cautious hope, I began to imagine myself there. Reclaiming my strength, one breath, one step at a time.

By the end of May, the fog began to lift. I felt better each day and I could think more logically and process thoughts. I decided to disconnect even more from Vic, taking back my energy. My thoughts of the ocean still lingered, craving that peace and healing of the salty air and sound of the crashing waves lulling me to sleep.

My friend Andrea and her boyfriend George agreed to backpack to the beach with me again for my annual trip. I was thankful I wouldn't have to go alone this year.

My pack lighter than the last trip, with food for one, Andrea, George, and I trekked down the beach to my favorite spot where we hung our hammocks in the trees.

We sat around the fire. George read aloud from a book, and Andrea and I enjoyed the story time.

George walked to the ocean while Andrea and I stayed by the fire. I felt the peace settle in. George came back and said, "You might want to go over to that piece of driftwood and look down."

I looked at him, confused. "What?" I laughed and studied his face.

He softly, slowly whispered, "You might have a friend who showed up."

I tilted my head to the side, furrowing my brow.

"Vic is here," he mouthed in a low whisper. "You didn't hear it from me, though."

Raising his voice again, George continued, "Just go look on the other side of that driftwood; there's a cool rock over there."

My heart rate quickened. I hated surprises; it always made my anxiety worse. Vic knew this. I was also done giving him my energy—he knew this as well.

Now what was I supposed to do? A year ago, I had solo camped on this very beach. This time, he drove the four hours alone and found my camp? I had hiked down that beach with every intention that I was done interacting with him.

I walked to the edge of the driftwood log and peered over the side. Vic lay on his back with his phone facing me, recording my reaction.

"I brought a cooler full of strawberry shortcake!" he exclaimed. "I wasn't sure if you were going to let me stay, so I left my stuff in the truck. I can go get it if it's okay if I stay."

"Sure. I'm sleeping in my hammock, but I have my tent with me. You can use that," I replied. I was annoyed, but I also felt bad that he'd made the effort to come visit and I didn't want to be mean.

He protested that he wanted to snuggle, but I held firm.

We watched the sunset and shortly after Andrea and George climbed into their hammocks. Vic and I sat in the sand; the glow of the fire lit up our faces as the salty air blew gently through. I worried about the campfire smoke that lingered around us. He was always clear about his allergy to campfires, so he never joined my backyard fires.

Abruptly, Vic unexpectedly kissed me, leaning against me and knocking me off-balance. I felt confused. Where was this coming from? He always refused to kiss me. Why now? Because I was mad at him? Because I was done? I suddenly felt self-conscious, knowing my friends were hanging in the hammocks only feet away from us.

"I don't want to lose you," he said with a fiery passion that seemed to come over him. "I love you."

This was the first time he'd said that to me, and something didn't feel quite right. I didn't know if I could trust it.

"Good night, Vic," I said as I stood before climbing into my hammock.

"Good night, Angie," he whispered with a hurt look on his face.

I had waited so long to hear those words. *I love you.* Words that once would have filled me with nothing but joy now landed differently. Tentative. Uncertain. Fragile.

My heart, wiser now, felt the shift, but also the hesitation. After so much waiting, so much hoping, he finally had sat beside me, offering what I had once begged for.

In the following weeks, he called me his girlfriend, he met my family, he pushed against the walls he had once hidden behind. And yet a small part of me stayed guarded, knowing that sometimes love is spoken because it is felt, and sometimes it is spoken because it is feared.

I walked forward, cautious but willing, learning that even long-awaited dreams come with shadows. And trust, like healing, is never built in a single moment. It's built step by step, breath by breath, heart by heart.

Chapter 23
Shifting Shadows

Two months after Vic surprised me at the beach, as July wrapped itself in heat and long evenings, I clung to the hope that maybe things were finally shifting. Vic agreed to join me for a backpacking trip, along with my best friend, Kristen, and her husband, Paul. A small, simple adventure that felt symbolic, like proof that we might finally be stepping into life together.

I had spent more than twenty years camping with Kristen and Paul, witnessing the quiet, enduring love between them. This trip was supposed to be the beginning of something new. But deep down, a quieter truth stirred. Sometimes things we hope will heal us only reveal how much still remains broken.

Kristen and Paul had arrived earlier in the day and described how to find them. "Follow the trail to the fork and then find the trail down to the small creek. Once you get to the creek, you might have to take off your shoes and walk across it, and then you'll be on a small island—that's where we'll be."

Across the creek, I spotted Kristen and Paul basking in the sun near the lake. Vic had my extra overnight pack on his back and his smaller daypack on his chest. It was only a couple-mile hike, so he said he didn't mind the extra weight, which included a toilet seat that he had strapped to his back.

"Hi!" I called to my friends, excited to see them.

"Hi!" they called back, standing for hugs.

"Hi, Vic, nice to meet you," Kristen said, smiling.

"Hi, nice to meet you too," Vic replied, looking around. He seemed nervous.

"Well, we'll set up camp and then join you for some sunshine," I told Kristen and Paul.

"Let's find another place to camp that's not close to your friends," Vic said once we'd stepped away.

I paused. "We're here to camp with them, so we aren't going somewhere else, but we can put some space between us."

Vic and I set up camp on the edge of the trees, a little ways from Kristen and Paul.

"Oh, I forgot my CBD drops in the Jeep, and I need them to be able to sleep tonight," Vic said. "I'm going to hike back to the Jeep."

"What? We just got here. Do you really need them?" I asked.

"Yes," he replied, grabbing his small pack and the keys to the Jeep.

"I'll go with you then," I said with a smile.

"No, you stay. Spend time with your friends," he said as he put his smaller pack on his back. "I'll be back soon."

After he left, I changed into my bikini and blew up a blue floatie chair I had packed, joining Kristen and Paul out in the water. I watched as Kristen and Paul swam in the lake. She looked happy, her shoulder-length brown hair and eyes glimmering. His strong yet gentle hand extended toward Kristen to help her onto a large rock that protruded from the lake. He swam, and she would follow; she swam, and he would follow. I looked on from my floatie, tethered to a nearby stump as their choreographed moves seemed so in sync. It was lovely to watch them. They were so tender toward each other and expressed so much love. I had watched them for years as our kids grew up, the quiet compassion they expressed in small ways. It warmed my heart and I thought, *That's the way life should be.* No relationship is perfect, but it wasn't about perfection; it was about acceptance, support, awareness of what the other person needed, and doing their best each day to be present.

A couple hours went by, and Kristen said, "We're going for a hike, want to come with us?"

"No, I'll wait here for Vic. He should have been back by now." I sighed. I had been watching the tree line, worried he may have gotten lost. At what point should I go look for him?

After they left to hike, I continued to drift in my inflated chair and pull myself toward my stump anchor only to let go and float out again. The bright sun made me squint. At least the sun didn't hurt my head like it had before.

Vic appeared at the edge of the tree line. "Hey!" he called with a wave.

"Are you okay? I was about to come find you. You've been gone for three hours!" I shouted toward the shore.

"I wasn't even gone an hour! I found the most amazing mossy creek on the way back; it was covered with rocks, and I was leaping from rock to rock. It was so amazing!" He seemed excited.

"Come on out and swim with me!" I shouted.

"Nah, I'm going to go back and look for more cool rocks!"

I felt my agitation grow. He had disappeared for three hours, and it was normal for him to lose track of time and not realize he'd been gone for hours. I would have gone rock hunting with him, but it would have been nice to know if he just wanted some time to himself.

He disappeared again to look for rocks, and I got out of the lake to change into dry clothes. An hour later, I could see him through the trees along the beach. I walked out to him, and we both looked at the rocks, sorting out the interesting ones, talking about the colors, shapes, patterns, and textures of the ones we liked. He'd been out for hours, and the sun began to set.

After sunset, we settled into my tiny backpacking tent. Vic began to dig frantically through his pack. "What are you looking for?"

"My sleeping pills," he responded.

"I'm sorry you have trouble sleeping without pills," I said.

I felt irritated because it always seemed to go the same way. The few nights we'd spent together, he wouldn't sleep, he'd take a sleeping pill or two, and then he'd continue to toss and turn all night, keeping me awake too. By the time he finally fell asleep, it was almost time for me to start my day at 4:00 a.m. I tried to be quiet, but he would be irritated by the slightest noise and scold me for being too loud when he was trying to sleep. I would feel sensitive and cry for how abrasive he was toward me paired with not having slept myself because of his sleeplessness.

In the tent, the sounds of the night started to soothe me. I had just drifted off to sleep when Vic woke me up as he began to thrash around on his sleeping pad, moaning.

"What's going on?" I whispered.

"Ooooooh," he moaned, "my legs, my legs are on fire, and my stomach hurts."

His body twisted as he moved and shifted, his back arched. "What do you need me to do?" I asked, worried. "Should I use my inReach to call for help?"

"No," he snapped, now on all fours in the tent.

"Did you eat something that was bad?" I asked, my mind searching to find a solution. We had eaten the same thing for dinner, but he didn't eat much of it. He was often disgusted by food and refused to eat anything.

"What about when you went to the Jeep earlier? Did you eat something there? Maybe you have food poisoning. I had that a few times before—it's miserable."

"No," he snapped again.

"You were gone for hours, I just wondered."

I couldn't figure out what could cause him so much pain.

"I'm going to hike out and get some help. I'm really worried about you," I said, but he protested.

I offered him the contents of my first aid kit. "Maybe a Pepto?" I held out a small pink tablet from my first aid kit.

For most of the night, he shifted his body, moaned, and held his stomach. He occasionally dozed off, only to wake moments later, seething with pain again. I drifted in and out of light sleep as I kept alert enough that if he needed something, I would be able to help.

He was in so much pain and would reject anything I offered to help.

The next morning, he finally slept, and as quietly as I could, I slowly unzipped the door of the tent and pulled my sleeping bag out with me, slipping out to walk to the shore of the lake. I fired up my Jetboil to boil water for my coffee. I nested myself inside my beach floatie and held my coffee cup under my nose, sipping slowly as I watched the sun rise.

Kristen woke up and made her way to my side. I told her that Vic had a rough night and I didn't know what to do, and let her know we would be leaving as soon as he woke up.

Vic felt too weak to hike his gear out, so I loaded both his gear and my gear into my pack. "Are you able to carry your body pillow out? It won't fit in my pack."

He nodded.

"Let's say goodbye to Kristen and Paul and we can hike out. Don't worry about anything; we can go whatever pace you're comfortable with. I've got you."

"No, I'm embarrassed and don't want to see them," he said.

"There's no reason to be embarrassed, you're not feeling well, and it's okay—they're the sweetest people I know."

Vic refused to say goodbye. He hung back in the trees as I moved toward Kristen and Paul. I turned to see Vic start down the trail toward the Jeep without me.

I asked Paul to help put my pack on. It weighed about sixty pounds and I appreciated the help lifting it onto my back. I shifted the pack back and forth, exhausted from the sleepless night, and I navigated to the trail, trying to keep up with Vic, who seemed much lighter now that we were away from camp and on our way back to the Jeep.

The trees, rocks, and lake revealed more than the landscape that trip. They showed me what was missing. Watching Kristen and Paul move together, with gentle looks, small touches, silent understandings, I saw, with painful clarity, the love I had been chasing but had never truly received.

Vic's spiraling descent followed swiftly. The squirming in the tent, the refusal to accept help, the anger that burned through tenderness like wildfire—all of it building into what I could only describe as Tornado Vic, a force that left destruction in its wake. I saw the rage, the struggle, the unchecked storm inside him, and anyone in his path felt the impact.

The sweet moments were no longer enough to tether me; they were crumbs scattered on a trail that led only deeper into confusion and darkness.

I carried more than the weight of our packs out of the wilderness that morning; I also carried the growing certainty that I was losing myself trying to hold on to someone who didn't seem to see me at all. As his moods twisted into spiraling storms, I realized that despite all my hope for peace and safety, I was standing too close to the center of the tornado—and if I stayed, it would crush me.

Chapter 24
Tender Departures

The rains came quietly at first, tracing lines down my windows like whispered sorrow. Outside, the last golden leaves of my favorite paper birch clung to the branches, trembling against the weight of winter's breath. Inside, I felt myself sink into darkness. The familiar heaviness of seasonal depression wrapped around me, and a slow burning in my chest warned that sickness might soon follow.

I listened to my body, to its pleading for rest. I made a batch of my old comfort "sick soup," spiced with garlic, turmeric, and ginger, letting the warmth fill the hollow spaces inside me. I burrowed into thick blankets, the world outside graying into cold and quiet. Hibernation was not just survival now; it was a necessity.

Still cocooned in my blankets, my phone buzzed. Vic's voice came through the receiver, urgent. "Angie, my dad was taken to the hospital. Will you come with me? You know I don't like hospitals." Exhausted as I was, I couldn't let him face it alone.

We navigated the sterile hallways, my mask damp against my face, my hands stinging with sanitizer. At Frank's bedside, the diagnosis came: liver cancer. I squeezed Frank's hand gently, our eyes locking in a heavy silence that spoke more than words. Memories of Nate flashed through me like ghosts riding the fluorescent lights above. I promised Frank, as I had once promised Nate, "Everything will be okay," even when the weight of that promise felt too big for my small, tired hands.

The next evening, I visited Frank again alone, not wanting him to be isolated in the sterile hum of machines. He asked about Nate's cancer, and I gave him the facts, watching him wrestle with regret and fear. "I'm thankful for you, Angie," he said, a tear slipping down his weathered cheek. I held onto his peace sign goodbye like a precious stone in my pocket.

Life, however, gave no space for grief to breathe gently. On the drive home, Vic called, frantic about Rocko, his small dog. Within hours, we were back in a hospital of a different kind—the emergency pet hospital. Rocko's liver was failing too. Vic spun into grief and rage, lashing at those trying to help. I stayed steady, offering what little strength I had left.

Rocko's decline was swift. I found myself lying with him through the night, whispering to him under the soft pink glow of fairy lights as Vic busied himself cleaning house. When the morning came, Rocko seemed fine, his arms crossed in front of him, looking at me. His tail swayed back and forth.

"You're such a good boy," I said, scratching his chin, and he seemed to smile at me.

Vic insisted Rocko wasn't acting right and had me drive back to the emergency vet. Insisting that Rocko was not well to the vet, Vic made the decision to let him go.

Vic, holding Rocko, swaddled in blankets, decided he was unable to be in the room. He quickly pushed Rocko's tiny body into my arms, stood and said, "I can't do this. You do it." and closed the door behind him. I was stunned that he would just leave the room. I silently cried, *No, don't leave me to do this alone! Why do I always have to be the strong one?*

I took a deep breath, whispering, "Such a good boy" as Rocko's final breath left his body, my tears soaking the blanket that wrapped him. I carried the weight of goodbye in my chest, the weight of being left alone again. I had to be the strong one, and I was tired of carrying this burden.

The next winter, Vic's father was slipping away too. Another message. Another summons. "He's dying. He wants you here."

I seemed to be in an eternal space of exhaustion for the last year. I couldn't catch up. It felt like one thing after another.

I put some leggings on under my pajama top and drove the short distance to his house under the suffocating black of winter's sky.

That night, with Vic's family gathered close, I sat by Frank's side, my hand resting on his heart as it stilled. It was the first time I had seen someone die. I struggled between anger that I had to witness it, the memory burning into my brain forever, and gratitude that I was able to bring love and light to the room.

Frank left this world the way he once told me he lived—slow and steady, riding his own ride, on his own terms. And while Frank found his peace, I realized I gave away every last reserve of strength I had. I wrapped the room in love, in tenderness, in light—but kept none for myself.

Grief was no longer a sharp stab; it had become a wide, heavy river rushing through every part of me. It was the exhaustion of carrying others through their storms while my own walls crumbled quietly inside. It was the silent winter after all the leaves had fallen, when the earth seems barren but is only sleeping—holding on, just barely, for spring's promised return.

Chapter 25
Tender Ground

As the new year approached, I carried more than just exhaustion. Grief clung to me like morning frost, dull and heavy, weighing down the first breath of 2020. New Year's Eve was a quiet sigh, and I was asleep by nine. I had hoped that with winter's end, the darkness would lift. That spring would bring some soft new beginning. But even as the days stretched longer, the ache lingered, and I knew something deeper needed tending.

Vic and I had finally admitted what had long been obvious: We were better as friends. "You should start dating other people," he said lightly, offering to help me set up a dating profile. I rolled my eyes, but inside, I felt a small, unfamiliar lightness. The pressure that had weighed us down was gone. Maybe, just maybe, I could start again.

By March, I threw a tropical-themed bunko night, craving connection and warmth. Sixteen friends filled my home with laughter and hugs, Ruby trotting between them wearing a tiny sombrero and a silk lei. For a few blissful hours, the world outside—the news, the warnings—felt far away. We joked about a virus, took a group photo, unaware that it would be the last time we would all gather like that for a long, long while.

Spring crept in quietly, and with it, Alex. His nature photography caught my eye first, but it was the way he moved through the world with curiosity, adventure, and the outdoors that stirred something in me. We met for breakfast in a quiet town, sunlight spilling over our table, the scent of bleach hanging in the air, conversation flowing easily. There was warmth in his blue eyes, a steadiness I hadn't realized I was searching for. I felt possibility pressing at the edges of my carefully guarded heart.

But guilt gnawed at me. Vic still lingered in my life. We were only friends and had been for a while, but his presence was complicated. I reassured myself that Alex and I were only just beginning, only tentative steps. Conversations with him became longer, we video-chatted, and I felt a tiny flame inside me ignite. I peeked out from the walls of my battered heart, and paid attention this time. Taking it slow. Learning. Was this a fit? Was he expressing his true self? He loved nature, hiking, and backpacking. It seemed like he loved them more than I did, which seemed nearly impossible, but I was curious and excited to finally have someone who would hike and backpack with me. I just worried if I could keep up with him.

Still, when Vic witnessed me dancing, twirling, and singing one afternoon, he questioned what sparked my joy. His face fell at the mention of someone new, and my heart twisted in the familiar ache of old patterns, feeling responsible for his disappointment, even when it wasn't mine to carry.

And then the world shifted beneath our feet. Lockdowns. Fear. Isolation. The pandemic unraveled any illusion of certainty, and inside that unraveling, my own wounds surfaced, raw and exposed.

Small, innocent moments with Alex would trigger the shadows of my past, the bracing for hurt, the expectation of abandonment. He hadn't caused these wounds, but still, I bled them into the spaces between us. I had lived so long starved of emotional safety that when genuine kindness arrived, I didn't know how to hold it. I questioned it, flinched from it, doubted my own worthiness of it.

In my thirst for love, I had forgotten how to trust that it could be real. And so, even as Alex showed patience, I found myself pushing him away, believing I wasn't ready. Believing I would only break something beautiful if I tried to hold it with hands still trembling from my past.

"I'm not feeling this," I texted him, though the truth was messier: I wasn't ready to feel anything at all.

Spring gave way to summer, and I returned to the simplest roots of friendship as the world around me felt fearful. I needed some comfort of the familiar, and Vic showed up at my door every day. We walked long miles apart but together, six feet of distance between us, speaking of fears and hopes in a world turned upside down. There was no pressure, no promises. Just simple presence. And maybe, in that stripped-down season, that was all either of us could give or receive.

Still, Alex remained in the corners of my mind—a soft ache, a whisper of what might have been. I wondered sometimes if I had let something real slip through my fingers. Or maybe I had made the right choice for the season I was in—the season where healing, not loving, had to come first.

Chapter 26
Healing Miles

Summer arrived unevenly, with the world in and out of lockdown, each week blurring into the next. I sat on the cold examination table in my doctor's office, wrapped in a flimsy gown that gaped at the sides, a thin shield against the vulnerability I felt. My doctor scribbled notes in my file, her face unreadable.

"The cyst needs to be removed," she said finally, glancing up. "It looks precancerous. It's grown to about five centimeters. That's about the size of a lime."

I instinctively placed my hand on my stomach, trying to imagine a lime-sized cyst on my ovary. Wondering if the tightness I'd felt lately came from too many stress-induced baked desserts, or the silent growing cyst inside me. The answer really didn't matter. My body had been sending signals for months. I was just finally listening.

My doctor wrote something in my chart. "Looks like surgeries are back on now, so you need to get this done right away," she said.

"I can't right now," I said.

She looked up at me. "Why not?"

"I have a backpacking trip planned in a few weeks. I've been training for it for the last couple months," I said as I sat up.

She put down the chart. "Tell me about this backpacking trip."

"Well . . ."—I hesitated, not wanting to tell her—"I'm hiking the Wonderland Trail." I smiled nervously.

"And how far is that?"

"Well, it's about ninety-three miles and 22,000 feet of elevation gain over eight days." I held my breath. "I need to do this."

"Okay," she said, "just know that this could rupture at any time, and you need to be fully aware that it could happen when you're out on the trail, but I guess since you are in otherwise good health and you've been training for it, I will say go ahead. Just listen to your body, and let's get you on the schedule for when you are off trail."

"Okay," I responded. "I will listen to my body and cancel if I need to."

"Good, stop at the appointment desk on your way out," she said, closing my chart and exiting the room.

I stood and removed the exam gown and put on my own clothes. I thought about my upcoming hike and how I had been looking forward to it before the permit had even been offered to me by a friend. I craved some deep nature time, immersing myself in the forests and basking in expansive mountain views. I reassured myself, *I'll be okay, I've got this. I'm going to hike the Wonderland Trail, and it's going to be epic!*

The anticipation of hiking the Wonderland Trail had sparked a fire under me and gave me something positive to focus my attention on.

I had been running every morning, starting small and working my way up in mileage, despite my hatred for it. I felt accomplished and determined as my body got stronger. My mind was clearer, and I felt more emotionally stable.

My cyst occasionally felt like a nuisance, with small pains here and there, but I monitored how I felt as I increased my activity since my last appointment.

Three weeks before Wonderland, on a Saturday morning, I had
some extra time and decided I would try to run farther than I had
before. I took a new route and as I pushed past five miles, I pushed
myself another mile, then another. I was over eight miles in and
tried to figure out the best way to get home over a now busy morning
road without a sidewalk. I ran along the edge of the country road and
when I saw a vehicle approach, I stepped into the ditch. The angle of
my foot sent a sharp pain up my ankle; I winced from the pain and
waited for the vehicles to pass. I carefully stepped back onto the road
and placed my foot flat, then I put pressure on my foot and lifted it. I
created a circular motion with my ankle to see how it felt—definitely
sore but it felt okay. I continued down the road, wincing as the pain
increased, determined to make it ten miles. I had never run ten miles
before. I turned down a road to take the longer way back and soon
realized I should have gone straight home. I could feel the electric
shocks of pain shooting up my ankle and it was tender to the touch.

As I entered my house and removed my shoe and sock, I saw my
ankle had already started to swell and bruise. My brow furrowed
and I let out a grumble. This was not my first sprain. I immediately
began the RICE method of treatment—rest, ice, compression,
and elevation.

With three weeks to trail time, I thought about the seventeen-
mile days with the extreme elevation gains and descents. I had
to laugh. A cyst, a sprained ankle, and recently I had an MRI
and learned I had torn meniscus in both knees. What else could
go wrong?

The next day, as I walked to the kitchen, I had a spasm in my
lower back. Worried that it was my cyst, I stopped. I evaluated how I
was doing and assumed that it was likely my modified gait trying to
baby my sprained ankle. I called my chiropractor, and they offered
me a massage and chiropractor visits back-to-back over the next
week.

As I was lying on the couch at home, icing my back and ankle, I got a text message from my friend who was the permit holder for the trail. "We've got a family emergency and need to back out of the hike."

"Oh no! I'm sorry," I replied. I felt disappointed. This was a bucket list hike, and I had been saving up vacation time at work for eight years for something like this. She offered me the permits if I could find someone else to go with me.

I wondered if the universe was putting so many obstacles in my way as a sign that the timing wasn't right or if it just wanted to see how badly I really wanted it. Was this a test of my determination, or was I being stupid to continue to try to find someone at the last minute to go with me?

This is happening for me, not to me, I told myself. *I've wanted to make this happen for so long.* I was going to keep trying.

Despite the medical challenges and being the last person left in the Wonderland permit group, I considered going by myself. I knew I could do it alone but decided that with the unknowns of my medical conditions, I should find others to hike it with me.

I sent out messages to a handful of people who I thought could take over the rest of the permits, including my cousin, Alex and my friend Marilyn. It was short notice, so it was too difficult to get time off work for some, and others had different plans or permits.

My friend Marilyn confirmed that she was able to move her calendar around and hike the Wonderland Trail with me.

Marilyn and I met at the Sunrise trailhead, the early morning sky a dark blue as the sun gave its first light, Mount Rainier's snow-covered mass contrasting against the sky. Bright stars still lingered and quickly disappeared as the blue hour dissolved into the golden hour, the sky a lovely glow just before the sun gracefully made its daily debut over the mountains.

"Marilyn!" I shouted as she stepped out of her car. "Are you ready to go for a walk?"

"Angie!" she chirped back. "Yesssssss! Are you?"

"Yes!" I danced in place, my pack bouncing on my back.

I had carefully weighed each item in my pack to make sure I only had what I needed and nothing more. I knew any extra weight on my body could slow me down or injure me more.

I had carefully wrapped my ankle with vet wrap that morning, and my knees were both swaddled with KT Tape and knee braces. My back was still a little stiff, but that also felt a lot better. "Good to go!" I told her, smiling as we walked to the trailhead.

I took a deep breath as I looked at the first hill in front of us. "The journey of a hundred miles starts with a single step," I said as I took the first step, and then another.

For eight days we woke in the dark and drank coffee and meditated while swinging in our hammocks. We spent early mornings hiking the gorgeous trail, the golden light of the day giving way to second breakfasts perched at a viewpoint, and found ourselves crossing rivers and meandering down the trails surrounded by wildflowers, eating our lunch along flowing water so we could replenish our water supply. As dinnertime approached, we would climb the final wooden steps that always seemed to indicate the arrival at our next camp for the night. In the evenings, we would hang our hammocks again, make dinner, and relish the last hours of daylight lounging, drawing, writing, reading, or swimming. We enjoyed seeing animals and nature, bushes filled with huckleberries bursting with flavor smelling of hot pie in the sun.

Over the course of hiking a total of 110 miles with side trails and detours, my body felt capable, tired, energetic, and overjoyed at the opportunity. The last uphill climb from the White River tested me. I paused more frequently; the toll of the last eight days had caught up with me. As we reached the top of the hill, my body felt stronger, and

I felt like I was on top of the world. I saw Mount Rainier in my face again, as it had often been along the journey around it.

Out on the trail, there was no pandemic, there was nothing I needed to do or take care of, I could just immerse myself in the present moment, savoring each and every one, reminding me that I loved life.

As I took my final slow steps toward my Jeep, I raised my hands above my head with my trekking poles outstretched and yelled, "*I love life!*"

I lowered my arms and giggled, looking at Marilyn as she did the same.

"Good job, friend," I said to her.

"Good job, friend," she replied.

Obstacle after obstacle rose up before me that summer—health scares, uncertainty, fear—but still, I pressed forward. There were moments when I questioned whether the universe was warning me to back down, to play it safe. But each time, I came back to the same truth: I didn't want to live small. I didn't want to shrink from life. I wanted to lean in.

In total, 110 miles of brutal, beautiful earth under my boots. Each step stripped away the noise of the world: the pandemic, the appointments, the what-ifs. Out there, among ancient forests, glorious mountain views, and open skies, there was only the next breath, the next step, the next summit.

I didn't feel broken out there. I didn't feel sick. I felt alive. Empowered. Whole.

Looking back, I am deeply grateful I made the decision to hike when I did.

The memories of the trail still vivid, on my doctor's recommendation I went in for a simple outpatient procedure to remove my cyst. It turned into something much larger. I awoke in a hospital bed, my stomach stitched with a long incision, the doctors explaining that they had found and removed extensive stage 4 endometriosis— tissue tangled deep inside me, unseen and silently growing possibly for over twenty years. They feared it might be cancer.

The C word again.

After the tests and the waiting and the sleepless nights, the words came back: no cancer. Just the long, slow work of healing.

The Wonderland Trail had been my victory lap before I even knew the battle I was about to face. And standing on the other side of it all, I realized that life doesn't wait for perfect timing. You have to say yes—to the trail, to the breath, to the fight for your own joy. While you still can.

Chapter 27
Stolen Safety

That dark season brought storms fiercer than I had ever known. Grief and exhaustion crashed over me like relentless waves, and through it all, Vic clung to me, desperate and drowning, pulling me deeper into his chaos.

He screamed at me again and again, *"Help me!"* But when I asked how, he only shook his head, insisting I already knew. His pain became a black hole, and no matter how much light I poured in, it wasn't enough. I was drowning right beside him, flailing in waters far too deep.

"No, no, no. You *know* what I need," he urged.

I sighed. "I can't read your mind, Vic. What do you need me to do? How can I support you?"

He raised his voice, shouting again into the phone, "Help me!"

"What can I do to support you, Vic?" I tried hard to remain calm.

"Help me! Help me! Help me! Just fucking help me!"

"Okay, I'm coming over there," I responded.

"No! Do *not* come over here!" he said.

"How can I help you if you won't tell me what I can do, and if you won't let me come over there?"

"You know!" he said.

"No, I don't know, or I would be helping you right now! I'm so tired and I don't know what you need. We are all grieving. I'm feeling depleted and worn out. I don't have much to give right now, but if you could just tell me what you need, I would sure like to try to help." I sighed again. My stomach, stapled from my surgery, I was supposed to be resting. I had been feeling the heavy grief of Frank's death, Rocko, the compounded grief from Nate's death and friends lost, and the chaos of the pandemic. Vic was struggling in deep grief. I tried to do what I could, and what I did do was never enough for him.

Our conversations would end with him hanging up on me, frustrated that I couldn't read his mind.

He talked excessively about taking handfuls of pills, wanting to kill himself, or about the guns in his house and seeing if he could hold one to his head. He sent me videos of him in his car inside his garage, the engine running, his face red from crying, telling me goodbye. He had sent me another video of him holding a plastic water bottle that held a small amount of liquid at the bottom. "You need to help me, or I'm going to drink the contents of this bottle." His face changed; a mischievous grin momentarily flashed before I saw the distress. I called 911 for wellness checks on him, afraid for his life.

I wanted to help him, but when I would show up at his house, he'd be locked in his bedroom yelling, "Get the fuck out of my house!"

"I need space," I said to him over the phone one afternoon. "I know you're struggling, but we're both drowning. I'm not a strong swimmer right now and you're trying to latch onto me when I can't even hold myself up."

"Nope, this is not happening. I'm coming over," he said. "We're going to talk about this."

"We keep talking about this, and I don't know what I can do. I'm exhausted. You're constantly talking about death, dying, and killing yourself. It is so triggering, and I'm crying all the time. I'm stressed and struggling so much; I just need some space so I can catch my breath!" I felt the ache in my bones from the weight I had been carrying. It was crushing me, and I knew that he couldn't help himself, let alone help me. I felt guilty for disconnecting, worried that if I wasn't there for him, he would kill himself and it would be my fault. Brandie had reassured me that nothing he did was my fault. It was on him. All I could do is make the calls to 911 when he threatened his life, and not take it on myself to make the wellness checks.

"Please," I whispered, "I just need some space. I need to take care of myself. I am exhausted."

"You haven't seen exhausted yet," he shot back, his words a whispered threat.

I hung up the phone and prayed that he would just let me have some space.

I slept on and off for the next few days, snuggled into my bed under a pile of blankets and a quilt, trying to get some of my energy back. Ruby cuddled sweetly against me; I heard her automatic pet feeder dispensing her food three times a day and the occasional sound of the pet door flap as she let herself out to potty. The house was quiet; the phone was silent. I heard the occasional *boom boom boom* of Vic's car. I knew he did it to let me know he was there, driving past my street, volume up, taunting me. Each time I heard his car, my heart rate spiked, my hands tingled, and I held my breath. I hated that car.

I lay quietly in my bed, my hand gently stroking the top of Ruby's head, scratching her chin and ears. It was dark outside, and my fairy lights strung between the birch trees created a gentle light in my second-floor bedroom. I took a deep breath; my body began to relax.

The doorbell rang and my heart rate spiked. Vic popped into my mind. I had asked him for space and told him not to come to my house, and I hadn't heard from him for days. Was it him?

I quietly but swiftly walked down the steps; my bare feet touched the soft carpet of the stairs until I reached the bottom. The hardwood floor was cold under my feet as I quietly tiptoed to the door to look out the peephole. I couldn't see anyone. I peeked behind the blinds from the office and still couldn't see anyone. Then I opened the front door slowly, holding Ruby back so I could get a better look. There had been other times the doorbell had rung and no one was there. Maybe it was just some neighborhood kids playing around. I shut the door and locked the dead bolt, and I heard a familiar noise behind me as I turned. I stopped. What was that?

My heart thumping loudly in my chest, I held my breath to try to make out the sound. *Calm down, heart,* I thought. *I need to know what that sound is.*

It was coming from the dining room. Ruby ran toward the sound, and I started running too as I realized it was coming from the dog door. I grabbed Ruby's collar to stop her as I saw a hand reach through the dog door and tap the floor and I heard whistles and tongue clicks, as if to say, *Come here, doggie.*

I scooped Ruby into my arms and covered her snout to keep her quiet. I ran up the stairs, stumbling with her, and watched as a flashlight shone through the living room curtains. When I entered my dark room, I saw the flashlight beams hit my bedroom window with the open curtains. I quietly closed my bedroom door and locked it behind me. I pushed through the walk-in closet door and closed the door after me, knowing that any light from my phone couldn't be seen. I shook, my heart thumping loudly in my ears. Why would they ring the doorbell only to go into the back gate, and why was someone's hand coming through the dog door? Was someone trying to hurt Ruby? Why was this happening? My iPhone clutched in my hand, I tapped the phone icon and dialed 911.

"911, is this an emergency?"

"Yes, there is someone in my backyard," I reported.

I told them what I knew, and they said they would send an officer right away and to stay where I was.

Soon after, they let me know that an officer was on the property.

My doorbell rang, and I saw it was a police officer. I stood in the doorway wearing a black nightgown with an oversized knit sweater on top, my feet bare. He said he'd checked the property and didn't see anyone in my backyard and asked if it could have just been the flashlight of someone walking their dog around the neighborhood.

"No, my doorbell rang and then I quickly got down here. There was no one here, but then there was a hand coming through my dog door. I *saw* the hand, and someone *whistling* for my dog!"

He looked surprised. "Do you know anyone who would do that?"

"Well, I don't know for sure because I didn't see anyone. It's possible that it could have been my ex. We're just friends now but not talking currently, so I don't know."

"That doesn't sound like a good friend if that's who it was."

"You're right, it doesn't," I said.

"Well, there's no one here now. If it happens again, please don't hesitate to call us."

I closed the door. I felt scared to be alone in the house. I picked up my phone and texted my friend Jack who lived close to me. I knew he had been at work and should be traveling home about now.

"You on your way home?" I texted.

"Soon, what's up?" he replied.

"I had a scary night. Could you come pick me and Ruby up and let us sleep on your couch?" I asked.

"Of course, are you okay?"

"Yes, I will be. I just need to sleep somewhere else tonight, and in the morning I'll go over to my mom's. It's so late, I don't want to wake her."

"I will be there as soon as I can," he replied.

I felt relieved to have friends like Jack. I gathered a few things in a bag and put the barrier on the dog door. It was the first time I had ever felt scared to stay in my own house.

The next day, I woke up on Jack's couch, and he handed me a cup of coffee. I told him about my evening and caught him up on recent events before walking down the road to my mom's.

The night the intruder reached through the dog door, terror became something real, something I could feel scraping against my skin— the lingering feeling of calling 911, my voice shaking, my heart hammering against my ribs. I didn't know then that it was Vic's hand reaching through. Only that my sanctuary had been shattered. My home, once a refuge, no longer felt safe.

Later, when he confessed, it was almost casual. An admission twisted with denial. "You're overreacting," he said, as if my fear was the problem, not his actions. As if the violation of my home, my peace, my safety, was just another thing I needed to swallow.

He promised he would never hurt me or Ruby. But the damage was already done. It wasn't bruises I carried; it was the invisible fracture of trust, the creeping, gnawing fear that no apology could undo.

I realized that survival wasn't just about facing storms outside; it was about learning to walk away from the storms that disguised themselves as friends.

Chapter 28

Silver Beginnings

Another summer rolled in, bright and heavy with the scent of possibility. Sunshine stretched across longer days, and yet, sitting at my desk, I found myself deep in reflection. Life looked nothing like I had once imagined. The storms of grief had changed me; the passing seasons had stripped me bare. And yet the call to live fully, to chase the short, fleeting wonder of life, was louder than ever.

I had been dreaming of tiny living long before the world unraveled. I collected floor plans like souvenirs, built Amazon wish lists overflowing with compact kitchen tools and foldable furniture. Downsizing, simplifying, wandering—it had always whispered to me. After months of working from home, I realized I didn't have to stay tethered to one place. Freedom had been waiting all along.

After careful analysis, complete with a wall of color-coded sticky notes, I made the decision: Sell the house. Start fresh. Choose adventure.

But dreams, even beautiful ones, often come with grief. Sorting through thirteen years of a life built inside those walls—Max's childhood laughter, late-night talks with Nate, family gatherings, celebrations, heartbreaks—it wasn't just physical work. It was emotional excavation. Every drawer, every closet, was a doorway to memory.

Still, I pressed forward. Less stuff, more life. That was the promise I made to myself. And somewhere in the mess of boxes and heartache, I found excitement building.

Offers on tiny homes fell through. The housing market burned hotter than I could chase. When my house sold in one day, I knew I'd have to pivot. A temporary home. A new idea. An RV.

Mom and I spent a Saturday trailing through dealership lots, paper coffee cups in hand, optimism thin but determined. I stumbled onto a silver Airstream Bambi by accident. It was small, perfect, glinting in the light like a silver promise. It wasn't the Basecamp I had imagined; it was better. I loved the separate sleeping space and workspace. I imagined myself working at the dinette and retreating to the bed for lunchtime naps.

I told the saleswoman I would wait until Tuesday. If it was meant to be, it would still be there. On Tuesday, it waited for me. A match with my silver Jeep. A strange, tiny symbol of resilience and new beginnings.

Settling into Bambi was not seamless. Learning systems, shrinking my life into 100 square feet, parking beside my mom's garage—it was messy, overwhelming, and often lonely. But every evening, as the walnut tree's leaves turned color and fell around me, I found small comforts in my new world. I learned how to be alone differently—more tenderly.

I hadn't expected the grief to find me again, but it did. Letting go of my home, of the memories it cradled, of the life I thought I would live—it was another kind of death. Another loss. Another surrender to change.

But I had made this choice. I had chosen to lean in. To believe that freedom was worth the ache of letting go. To trust that sometimes, even when the ground feels shaky, you are exactly where you need to be.

Chapter 29

Tattered Wings

Winter settled thick around my tiny Airstream, blanketing the world in a heavy hush. Inside, a different kind of storm raged: grief, confusion, betrayal, and the desperate longing to heal. Just when I thought I was beginning to mend the tattered edges of my heart, Vic appeared again, unexpected and uninvited, at my door. A ghost from the life I was trying to leave behind, standing in the dark with apologies and promises I had heard too many times before.

The past, it seemed, was not done with me yet. And neither was the work I still had to do to save myself.

One night, parked at the side of my mom's garage, a knock echoed on my Airstream door. I expected it to be my mom, but when I opened the door, I found Vic standing there in the dark, leaning against a bicycle. I hadn't seen him in months.

Hands raised in surrender, he said, "Please know you're safe. I just wanted you to know I'm okay. I'm getting healthy. I'm happy."

His face was different—fuller, softer. His eyes held a calm I hadn't seen in years. Against the cold ground under my bare feet, I felt a flicker of curiosity. I could have sent him away. Maybe I should have. But I didn't.

Inside, seated at my small dinette, he confessed.

"I've been using methamphetamine . . . for the last three years."

The words hung between us like smoke.

He spoke of detox, meetings, healing. He beamed about small victories, gaining weight, riding his bike, waking up happy.

I sat stunned, the pieces of our past sliding into place: the bloody noses, the erratic moods, the spirals, the weight loss, the sleepless nights. All the ways I had blamed myself for things I never could have controlled. It all made sense now. Meth had been the unseen third party in our relationship for most of its life.

That night, I lay awake in my tiny bed, anger and betrayal churning inside me. I had let him drive Ruby and me around while he was using meth. I had loved him, trusted him, while he lived a lie.

I reached for my phone and emailed Brandie: "Do you have any available therapy slots ASAP? I could use an extra session." It was an email she had received from me often over the last several years.

In the weeks that followed, Vic answered my questions. He apologized. He acknowledged the damage he had caused.

"Can we be friends again?" he asked.

I hesitated.

"Maybe. But I don't know who you are without meth."

He flinched at the word. He didn't like when I said it out loud — meth. He insisted he was still the same person he'd always been. But I wasn't so sure. I had seen both Dr. Jekyll and Mr. Hyde. And while I wanted to believe the version sitting in front of me now — clearer, softer, repentant — I also couldn't forget the version who had terrified me.

Maybe it wasn't him who scared me. Maybe it was the addiction — the grip it had on him, how it twisted his moods, rewrote his truths, turned love into chaos. That realization hadn't quite formed yet, but it was beginning to take shape. And it would matter. Because understanding the difference between the person and the addiction would change how I processed the pain he left behind.

Just days after those interactions, work handed me a new assignment: writing a textbook on substance use disorder. As I dug into research, worked with experts, and read scientific journals, I learned the very language I needed to understand a topic I had no experience with.

It wasn't "meth addict." It was "someone with substance use disorder."

It wasn't a moral failing. It was a brain disease that hijacked behavior, memory, and self-control.

I found compassion. And I built stronger boundaries.

Vic and I spent occasional time together. We laughed; we remembered how easy it once had been. But beneath it all, I kept my walls intact.

Sometimes he joked about marriage.

"Someday," he said, "someday we'll get married."

But someday had been dangled before me too many times already.

When I traveled in my Airstream, he'd text: "Thinking about coming to see you."

And sometimes he would. Sleeping on the folded-down dinette, staying a few days. Bringing both comfort and the old familiar pull I fought hard not to fall back into.

By late summer, I parked my Airstream under towering beach trees on the coast. I booked a solo whale-watching tour. I watched the waves roll in and found peace in the way the earth moved without asking anything of me.

Vic texted again: "Thinking about coming to see you."

I was tired of words without action. I had to set a new boundary.

"If you come, please get your own campsite or a hotel."

He responded: "That's too much work. I'll think about it."

Later that day, he sent me selfies from the coast—five miles away from me—never coming to my campsite, never explaining. A cruel echo of five years of broken promises and a "fuck you" to my boundary.

I threw another log onto my fire that night, and when his text finally came ("Made it to Salem. Sleep good."), I realized I was waiting for someone who was never coming.

Not really.

And maybe never had been.

In the weeks that followed, grief flattened me. A dark night of the soul descended. I journaled, I cried, I unraveled the cords of my past. The childhood wounds, the fear of abandonment, the desperate need to be chosen. I realized how hard I had tried to be enough for people incapable of loving me the way I deserved.

I curled into my Airstream's rear bed as the rain pattered on the aluminum roof, feeling small, raw, broken.

Suicidal thoughts flickered at the edges of my mind, full of shame, loneliness, regret. I suffered silently, too ashamed to tell even those closest to me. Everyone was relieved that Vic was gone from my life. No one understood the grief of losing someone toxic. The confusion, the lingering wounds invisible to anyone who hadn't lived them.

Then came the final betrayal.

Photos appeared online: Vic smiling with a new girlfriend, in places we had once stood.

Only weeks after telling me I was his soulmate. Only weeks after promising me "someday."

When he broke no contact to send me love songs, when he showed up at my door to tell me that "she's not you," it wasn't flattering. It was a knife twisting deeper.

He called me his treasure while building a future with someone else.

"No," I told him, "I will not be that person. I will not do that to her; I will not do that to myself."

I wasn't a treasure to him. He'd had five years of opportunity. He wasn't going to tell me I was his soulmate when it took him a minute to express his devotion to someone else.

I was a safety net he reached for when he was scared.

I had been telling myself for so long: I deserved better.

A week later, he FaceTimed me from the airport, flashing a ring on his left hand. "It's just repellent," he said.

I knew I was witnessing the end of the delusion I had carried for far too long.

I told him to never contact me again.

And for once, I meant it.

Our final conversation broke something clean inside me—the last fragile thread tying me to the fantasy I had held on to for far too long.

It was never about my worth. It was never about being good enough, patient enough, loving enough.

It was about him never being ready, and me finally being ready to let go.

I wasn't a second choice. I wasn't the "maybe someday." I wasn't the backup plan, the almost, the could-have-been.

I was the butterfly still unfolding her wings, aching but alive, fragile but free.

It was time to fly away from what hurt, toward the life I was meant to live. Not for someone else. Not to prove anything. But because I finally realized: I was always worthy of being loved, fully and without conditions—starting with myself.

Chapter 30
Becoming Light

After six long months wrapped in grief, after the harshest emotional winter I could remember, something shifted. A familiar ding echoed above me, pulling me from sleep.

Through the soft edges of my silk eye mask, I saw light. Faint and promising. My body ached, my throat was dry, and every muscle felt like it carried the weight of too many seasons. I slowly lifted the mask, adjusted the N95 stretched across my nose and mouth, and turned toward Melinda. Her eyes were tired, but her smile was soft and steady. I remembered our trip to Iceland; I loved that we traveled well together.

"I'm so exhausted," she whispered.

"Me too," I agreed, the corners of my mouth lifting.

I pressed the button on the seat back in front of me, the airplane map glowing. So close to Denpasar, the capital of Bali. Estimated arrival: 11:55 p.m. I stretched my arms over my head and leaned into the cool window, feeling the hum of the engines underneath my bones.

Two months earlier, Melinda had called me, her voice urgent, a lifeline. "I need a spiritual retreat," she'd said.

Without knowing it, she saved me. The promise of Bali had kept me alive when the darkness threatened to swallow me whole. It had been the ember of light I clung to when everything else had gone dark. And now, carried across oceans by the wings of an airplane, I was finally ready.

Ready to be nurtured.

Ready to emerge.

The villa unfolded like a dream, lush gardens, narrow turquoise pools, the scent of flowers on warm air. Twelve women gathering at just the right time, each carrying invisible bruises, each seeking something they couldn't yet name.

The first morning, before dawn, I stumbled down the dark stairs of my villa. Clumsy, hopeful, only to fall hard, striking my head against marble and dislocating a toe.

Not the start I had imagined. But maybe exactly the start I needed.

Pain and healing wove themselves together. A trip to the hospital. A splinted toe. A reshuffled itinerary. And a deeper surrender to trust the path, even when it bent in unexpected directions.

Two days later, dressed in flowing traditional Balinese attire, I stood at the sacred temple of Tanah Lot under the dark "black moon." The timing felt divine. A rare lunar phase signaling endings and beginnings. A perfect mirror for where I stood in my life.

The salty sea breeze lifted my hair as I placed flowers in prayer, following the cues of the high priest. The bells were ringing while he splashed me with holy water and stuck rice to my forehead. I released everything. The heartbreak. The self-doubt. The endless waiting to be chosen.

In the gentle smoke of incense, in the cool spray of the ocean mist, surrounded by flowers, I released the shell of my cocoon and set intentions for my wings that would emerge. I was ready to become a butterfly.

Two days after my visit to the temple, I stood in the dark in what seemed to be the middle of nowhere. I rubbed my hands together, my red backpack over my right shoulder, a diagonal-cut sandwich in my left hand. I took a bite, the lettuce and cucumber moist against the whole wheat bread. I bounced lightly on my left foot; my hiking shoes felt tight against my split-covered toe. I was nervous as I looked at my new friend Elizabeth from the healing retreat and then over to our hiking guide, who handed me a bottle of water.

"Finish your food," he said as I stuffed the rest of the sandwich in my mouth, eagerly.

"Ready," I mumbled, my mouth full.

Our driver opened his door and waved. "See you when you get back."

"Sounds good, get some sleep," I told him.

It was 3 a.m. and Elizabeth and I had traveled an hour and a half from our villa to arrive at the trailhead for Mount Batur in Bali. It felt almost surreal to be there, the dark enveloping us, the stars bright overhead. I had come to Bali to find healing and to climb a mountain for sunrise. I was determined to make both happen.

Our guide Katut handed me a headlamp to cut the darkness. I declined and pulled my own headlamp out of my backpack, placing it on my head, and set the brightness to the second level—the familiar glow in the darkness.

"Wait here," said Katut.

We paused at the side of the road as he disappeared behind a fence and emerged with two walking sticks made from bamboo. I wished I had brought my trekking poles from home.

"First time hiking with a bamboo walking stick." I smiled, thinking it was neat as my hand gripped the top of the bamboo.

Katut led us to a small building with a wooden deck—"toilet," he said.

Propping my stick against the outside wall, I entered the large room with the porcelain toilet inset into the floor. Having heard about these toilets, I straddled the toilet and peed into the hole, the bucket of water beside me with the ladle to rinse the bowl.

"Ready," we said, as Katut led us to a narrow dirt path with grass on both sides as the path widened.

My headlamp lit up large banana leaves and ferns, and the smell of onions on the breeze startled me. I wondered for a moment if it was body odor.

"Smells like onions," I said as I shifted the weight of my pack on my back.

Pausing, Elizabeth agreed, "Oh! It does."

"Onions," Katut said as he pointed his headlamp to a field near the trail.

I turned my head to see the tall green growth of onion tops sprouting from the earth, my headlamp catching dewdrops that shimmered like opals.

As we turned from the wide path into the trees, I wondered about wildlife, if there were snakes or ticks and if I should have applied my mosquito repellent. Mosquitoes had been bad all week, and darkness paired with my headlamp seemed to beckon to them for a feast.

The trail steepened, and each step I took was intentional. I was careful with the placement of my foot to best support my cracked toe that still had the SAM splint on it inside my hiking shoe. I felt the discomfort of a hot spot at the back of my heel, the familiar feeling when a blister was forming. I considered the options. If anything were going to hurt, I would take a blister over pain in my toe.

THE SEASONS THAT SHAPED ME

Katut reached out his hand to help me up onto the lava rock. My ego considered brushing him off. The old me would have refused the help, not allowing myself to rely on anyone, needing to be strong, needing to do it all myself. Thinking somehow receiving help was taking away from my experience or making me weak.

Instead, I placed my hand in his and he pulled me up.

"Thank you," I said, grateful for the extra hand and that I'd given myself permission to allow the help.

My headlamp caught the pink color of the lava rock and acknowledged that I was climbing an active volcano. In the dark. I smiled as we paused on a flat spot.

"We have time, no rush," Katut said. "Rest."

I shifted my weight to my right foot and checked in with my toe, moving it slightly in my shoe. It felt slightly uncomfortable, but I was feeling more confident that I would make it to the top, although it was coming down that made me nervous. I looked out, away from the peak into the night sky, the silhouette of Mount Agung in the distance, a slight glow against the horizon. I turned off my headlamp and tilted my head back.

"Wow!" I exclaimed. "Look up."

Elizabeth tilted her head back and propped her hands on top of her bamboo walking stick, echoing my awe.

We stood, savoring the moment. I felt like the stars were twinkling in my eyes, and I could feel it in my heart.

As we climbed higher, I heard the earth waking and felt the tightness in my legs. A week of yoga and deep massages, after the stillness of the last several months of cocooning, suddenly came rushing in. A drop of doubt hit the stillness of my calm pool and rippled out; I felt the twinge in my toe. Worried I might let Elizabeth down on her first sunrise hike, worried I might let myself down, I had been wanting this summit.

Katut extended his hand again, navigating us through the small particles of scree. Each step forward, the scree slid beneath my feet, causing my body to slide backward slightly. Katut's hand pulled mine, helping me balance; as we continued our ascent we paused at a few small wooden shelters and benches built along the trail.

A faint light outlined the horizon and Mount Agung, expanding upward, washing out the stars that were so brilliant just moments before.

Katut paused at a long bench and rolled a blue pad along the bench. "Sit, I make breakfast."

"Okay," I nodded in the dark, my gaze on the horizon, afraid of missing a moment of the sunrise.

I removed my pack and placed it on the bench and sat next to Elizabeth. We took some photos and Katut reappeared with two steaming clear glass mugs of Balinese coffee. I sipped the hot black coffee, the steam carrying the smell of fresh coffee into my nose, savoring the flavor of that first sip.

I looked at Elizabeth. I could start to make out her red hair pulled into a messy bun, gentle curls falling around her beaming face as the pink-and-red glow of the sunrise peeked from behind the clouds. "Thank you for sharing the sunrise with me," I said.

"Yes! I'm so glad." I could hear her smile through her distinctive Texas accent.

I recalled that first hike memory from when I was five, sharing a cup of coffee with my dad. I recalled similar memories on hikes with others since then. I savored those moments, and here I was on top of a mountain in Bali with a new friend, sharing coffee.

Katut reappeared in front of us. "Breakfast," he said as he handed us a tray filled with food and placed it on the bench between us. I grabbed a diagonal-cut sandwich and took a bite, unsure of the contents. Hot banana smashed inside white bread. I was surprised that I liked it, the banana creamy and the white bread sticky. I finished off the sandwich half and grabbed an egg, startled that it was hot.

"Oh, it's hot!" I said as I tapped the egg on the wooden bench. I cracked the shell carefully, peeling it away, exposing the steaming, cooked inside.

"Oh, it is," Elizabeth responded as she tapped her egg.

We sat in silence, finishing our sandwiches, hot eggs, and fresh fruit that I had only recently discovered: rambutan and salak. I watched the sky light up and shivered; the heat created on the way up the mountain had faded. I pulled my gray thermal shirt over my gray tank top and added my new pastel T-shirt on top of that. My T-shirt read "Good Karma" in a raspberry pink, and I was channeling all the good karma I could.

"Come see the steam," Katut said, waving his hand toward us.

I was able to see his face for the first time; his kind eyes and dark hair were framed by the hood of his gray sweatshirt. He turned and walked away from us, and I noticed his black backpack that looked like it had seen many hikes, its edges frayed and color faded.

Katut led us up from our sunrise bench to a steaming hole in the ground. I placed my hand over the hole and felt the hot moisture against my hand. He handed me a stick of incense.

"Blow it into the hole," he said, pointing. "Bali magic."

I blew the incense into the hole, causing a plume of steam to overflow from the hole, enveloping me, and I giggled.

"I'm giving myself a facial," I said, then laughed as I blew again.

Katut explained that the steam hole was where they cooked the eggs and bananas for our breakfast.

"Amazing!" I exclaimed, not realizing that they had cooked the breakfast right there, using the volcano as an oven.

Katut led us to the rim of the volcano and sauntered along it as we alternated between reveling in the beautiful views inside the crater, the gorgeous morning light of the sunrise glow over the nearby villages.

I thought about the community I felt in Bali, the connections I had been missing in my life back home as I traveled alone. I thought about the loneliness I had felt traveling by myself for months at a time, not talking to another human. I thought about my life, about the losses and grief, and also about the amazing parts, the joy and the laughter, the family and friends who loved me. I thought about my dad and how much he had inspired me to climb mountains when I was a child, how much he had loved it until his Parkinson's made the mountains a memory.

I unlocked my phone and turned off the airplane mode to see if I had a signal. The bars on the top of my phone searched for a signal as I paused my step. *Ah! Signal!* I told Elizabeth and Katut that I would be a moment, that I was going to call my dad.

"Hey, Angie," my dad said when he picked up, "trying to find you." The screen was dark as he tried to turn on his video.

"Hi, Dad! I'm on top of Mount Batur in Bali!" I smiled at him as his video started, his face up close.

"Oh neat!" he replied, his voice excited.

There had been other times while I stood on top of other mountains that I had called him, knowing that he could no longer make the climb himself. I wanted to share these moments with him because his passion for the mountains ran deep, just as it did for me. I never wanted to take for granted that illness, injury, disease, and death can show no mercy and change our lives swiftly, drastically, and irreversibly from the life we hold so dear.

"Hang on." I smiled as I tapped my screen to flip the video around.

I gave him a tour of the top of Mount Batur, showing him the inside of the crater, the steam, the sun that was now warm above the horizon, the small buildings down at the base of the mountain.

I watched his face as I described each highlight and he smiled. I thought about how much I would have loved to hike with him again as I hung up the phone, feeling a swell of gratitude in my heart that I could at least call him.

I paused at the edge of the crater, the sun on my face. I closed my eyes and listened to the sounds of the birds carried in the gentle breeze. I took a deep breath, filled my lungs with the smell of the earth, the grass, the air, the flowers. I felt the warmth of the sun on my face as the pockets of cool breeze tousled my hair. I opened my eyes and carefully spun in a slow circle, wanting to remember this moment forever.

I felt my arms outstretch, my palms open. I imagined my wings unfold. I had felt myself emerge all week, and now, feeling the accomplishment of reaching my goal, I basked in the sun. I recognized that I had put my mind to this and I was able to make it happen. It gave me hope, and a pang of sadness. There is some sadness that comes with reaching a goal—for the losses along the way. I couldn't help but wonder if I had tried harder in the past, if things would have been different. Then I realized that I was always doing my best with what I knew at the time. Over time, there is growth and understanding, and I needed to trust that what was meant for me wouldn't pass me by, and if it did, it wasn't the right time, place, or people.

As I looked down the mountain at where I had come from, I thought about the peaks and valleys of my life, about how much beauty there had been in both the highs and the lows. I thought about how sometimes the people I believed would be standing at the peak with me weren't. I thought about the moments in my life when I'd fought against the challenges and made it to the top, about the hard seasons and how the shattered fragments of my experiences created a beautiful kaleidoscope of colors that captured the light.

I thought about how I stood here, in this moment. *This is where I will be reborn. On top of a volcano.*

Destruction.

Rebirth.

My eyes wide, the golden glow of the sunlight touched all the new life below me. I felt thankful I hadn't given up when life felt too hard. Life would go on, and I was determined to make it better than I could ever have imagined.

A butterfly does not mourn its cocoon. It honors it, the place of darkness and struggle that made flight possible.

All the heartbreak, the losses, the lonely seasons—they were not wasted. They had shaped me. Strengthened me. Colored me with the kaleidoscope of survival.

Standing on the rim of a volcano, nature's purest symbol of destruction and rebirth, I understood:

I was not here to stay small.

I was not here to keep waiting for someone to save me.

I was not here to stay tethered to old wounds.

I was here to rise. To fly. To love this life, no matter how it unfolded.

The breeze carried whispers of every season I had survived, seasons of loss, of love, of renewal.

I was not untethered from my past; I was untethered from the weight of it.

I had finally chosen myself. And this time, I would not fold my wings.

And so, with open hands and an open heart, I stepped forward. Ready for whatever season awaited. My story, like every season, was always meant to evolve. The season of waiting was over—it was time to bloom.

Epilogue

In the quiet reflection after the climb, I can see now that life has always been a series of seasons. The seasons that shaped me were never just about the passing of time. They were about the way life kept asking me to begin again. A journey of grief, healing, and learning to bloom again. Each chapter, each turn of the earth, carried its own lessons in loss, resilience, and hope. Through every season, I noticed a quiet thread woven through my life: perseverance. I crossed trails despite injuries. I climbed mountains on broken toes. I stayed too long in places where love faltered. All because I believed that if I gave enough, hoped enough, loved enough, it would somehow be enough.

Often I wondered whether the universe was warning me to let go or asking how deeply I was willing to believe in what I wanted. I am learning now that perseverance is a gift, but it's also a teacher. Not every mountain must be climbed. Not every dream requires losing yourself to chase it. Strength sometimes looks like holding on, but often it looks like knowing when to lighten my pack, turn around, or let go.

The Seasons That Shaped Me: A Journey of Grief, Healing, and Learning to Bloom Again is not just a story of survival; it's a story of becoming. Of trusting that even after the darkest winters, there will always be another spring. Of believing that it's never too late to begin again. And somewhere deep inside me, there will always be that soft, stubborn stirring toward the light. The seasons that shaped me are not just a memory; they're a promise. I will keep choosing life. I will keep choosing hope. I will keep choosing love. I will keep blooming.

And with every new beginning, I will carry forward the strength, the softness, and the courage that were forged in the seasons that shaped me.